THE BEATLES

Life with the Band

THE BEATLES

Life with the Band

Sandra Forty

CHARTWELL
BOOKS

This edition published in 2014 by

CHARTWELL BOOKS
an imprint of Book Sales
a division of Quarto Publishing Group USA Inc.
276 Fifth Avenue Suite 206
New York, New York 10001
USA

Copyright © 2014 by Greene Media Ltd.
34 Dean Street, Brighton BN1 3EG

DVD Licensed by Eagle Rock Entertainment

Jacket & Layout by Sunita Gahir, Bigmetalfish Design Services

ISBN-13: 978-0-7858-3130-3

Printed and bound in China

The Liver Building and seafront of Liverpool.

Contents

Introduction

John, Paul, George, and Ringo—collectively the most popular and influential rock and roll band that the world has ever seen. Individually, they each embody the ideal musician, let alone some of the very best ever singer-song writers. The 1960s and every decade since have been shaped by The Beatles and even now, fifty years on from their beginning, they remain one of the most respected and enjoyed bands of all time. Who would have thought it when they first emerged from the heartland of Liverpool—four skinny, young, likely lads—that they would go on to conquer the world? Not even they thought they would find fame much beyond the beat clubs of England and Germany, let alone last more than a couple of years.

The Beatles came to define their era in a way that no other band or performer has managed. The Beatles only lasted between 1962 and 1970, but in the course of their eight remarkable years they produced an astonishing thirteen albums of original, self-composed music, including at least two that invariably make every "all time great" chart listing. Their success was truly global and during their heyday and for some years after, they were four of the most recognizable faces on the planet: arguably they still remain so.

The statistics are amazing:
• 17 UK number one hit singles (using the official charts); 20 in the US (*Billboard*)—13 in common; 12 in Germany; 23 in Australia; 21 in The Netherlands; 18 in Sweden; 22 in Canada; 21 in Norway
• 69 weeks at number one

• Singles that spent 456 weeks on the charts
• the largest ever sale in one week (970,000) by a non-charity single
• the largest advance sale (1.4 million) by a non-charity single
• as of 1968 every Beatles' single had sold over one million copies; 26 had sold over one million in the US alone
• eight No.1 EPs
• 63 weeks at No.1; 132 in the US
• 392 total weeks on chart
• 15 No.1 albums in the UK; 19 in the US
• 175 total weeks at No.1
• 1,278 weeks on chart
• most weeks at No.1 in a year (40)
• first album to debut at No.1 (*Help!*)
• 45 total weeks simultaneously at the top of both album and singles charts
• 107 million album sales in the US
• 4.8 million sales by *Sgt. Pepper* in the UK
• seven Grammys
• 15 Ivor Novellos
• five albums in *Rolling Stone's* top 500 (*Sgt. Pepper* at 1, *Revolver* at 3, *Rubber Soul* at 5, and *The Beatles* at 10)
• total album sales worldwide to date: 2,303.5 million

▶ The Beatles were huge in the USA, selling a massive number of records and playing to packed audiences—so much so that stadiums had to be used, opening the way for the mega-concerts we know today. On stage Las Vegas, August 26, 1964. *Mirrorpix*

8

When The Beatles announced that they were going their different ways in 1970, their millions of fans were shocked and saddened: why had it come to this? The answer lies in the nature of their fame: their phenomenon had become so colossal that the instigators at its heart had become disillusioned and fractured by the experience. Brian Epstein had held them together and sorted out their differences but after he died they were anchorless and inevitably drifted in different directions.

Personal animosities were heightened by greater numbers of people joining their entourage and influencing them in different ways. They always denied any possibility of a reunion but by the time of John's untimely death it seems that personal bridges had been rebuilt and that they were largely able to forgive and forget the bad bits and remember—as we can—just how much they liked each other, what they meant to each other, and just how much of their time together had been magnificent.

◀ A wall of pin-up photos of The Beatles while they were the "Fab Four."

“I don't think anybody comes close to The Beatles.”

Brian May

THE EARLY YEARS

TO 1961

"I was wandering through the St.Pauli district of Hamburg and was suddenly attracted by the sound of Rock and Roll music. It was Rory Storm and the Hurricanes at the Kaiserkeller. The next group to appear were The Beatles. I was speechless!"

Klaus Voormann

◄ The Silver Beatles: Pete Best, George, Paul, and John.

Timeline

1926
January 3—George Martin born in Highbury, London.

1934
September 19—Brian Epstein born in Liverpool.

1940
June 23—Stuart Sutcliffe born in Edinburgh.
July 7—Richard Starkey born at 9 Madryn Street, Dingle, Liverpool.
October 9—John Winston Lennon born at Oxford Street Maternity Hospital, Liverpool.

1941
October 13—Neil Aspinall, born in Prestatyn, Wales.

1942
June 18—James Paul McCartney born at Walton Hospital, Rice Lane, Liverpool.

1943
February 25—George Harrison born at 12 Arnold Grove, Wavertree, Liverpool.

1950
George Martin takes job at Parlophone Records.

▲Left to right: George, John, and Tony Sheridan performing live onstage during The Beatles first Hamburg trip.

1954
September—Paul meets George on the bus home from their school, the Liverpool Institute High School for Boys.

1956
Julia buys John a mail-order guitar.

1957
Paul and George begin playing together. John starts a skiffle group that becomes The Quarrymen, named after the school most of the band attend, Quarry Bank High School.
June 22—The Quarrymen play their first gig—an Empire Day celebration from the back of a lorry.
July 6—John's friend Ivan Vaughan introduces him to Paul McCartney at the Woolton Parish Church Fete where The Quarrymen are playing.
August 7—The Quarrymen's first gig at the Cavern.
September—John starts at Liverpool College of Art.
October 18—Paul's first gig with

> ❝It was thought that The Beatles had gone to Hamburg as an old banger and had come back as a Rolls-Royce.❞
>
> *Johnny Hutchinson of*
> *The Big Three*

1960

May—Allan Williams becomes manager. Tommy Moore is recruited as drummer. They become The Silver Beatles.

May 5—the band auditions to back Bill Fury. His manager (Larry Parnes) books them to back Johnny Gentle.

May 20–28—the band tours Scotland supporting Gentle.

June 13—Tommy Moore leaves.

July—John leaves Liverpool College of Art.

July 9–23—Norman Chapman joins as drummer but doesn't work out.

July 24—Allan Williams arranges for Bruno Koschmider to see the band. He likes what he sees and invites them to Hamburg.

August—Pete Best becomes the new drummer.

August 17—The band, now named The Beatles, arrives in Hamburg and plays at the Indra Club.

October—Ringo is playing in Hamburg with Rory Storm and the Hurricanes and meets John, Paul, and George.

October 4–November 30—The Beatles leave the Indra for the

▼John and Paul in the Cavern Club c. 1960.

The Quarrymen at New Clubmoor Hall, Liverpool.

1958

February 8—George is introduced to John.

July 15—John's mother, Julia Stanley, is knocked down by a drunk driver and dies.

December 20—The Quarrymen play at Harry Harrison's (George's brother) wedding reception.

1959

January—life is tough for The Quarrymen, at one stage reduced to John, Paul and George, before they are joined by Stu Sutcliffe on bass.

Kaiserkeller where they play alongside Rory Storm and the Hurricanes. During their time at the Kaiserkeller they meet Klaus Voormann and his then girlfriend Astrid Kirchherr, and Jürgen Vollmer.

October 16—Koschmider signs The Beatles up for another stint to continue at the Kaiserkeller. They also jam with Tony Sheridan elsewhere.

November 1—Koschmider terminates the band's contract at the Kaiserkeller and they start moving from the Bambi-Filmkunsttheater cinema—their digs up till now—to a room above the Top Ten Club.

November 21—George is deported from Germany—at seventeen he's under age.

November 29—Paul and Pete Best are deported after an incident with a lighted condom, a farewell gift to Koschmider before leaving the Kaiserkeller for the Top Ten Club. They arrive in London on December 1.

December 10—John goes home but Stuart stays in Germany with Astrid Kirchherr.

December 17—First British performance as The Beatles, at the Casbah Coffee Club, Liverpool, which is owned by Pete Best's mother. Chas Newby plays bass. They are sensational.

1961

February—Pete Best asks Neil Aspinall to drive their van. He becomes the band's roadie.

April 1–July 1—The Beatles return to Hamburg to play at the Top Ten Club where they are occasionally joined on stage by Stuart Sutcliffe.

June 1—John's (Cynthia) and Paul's (Dot Rhone) girlfriends visit.

June 22—Bert Kaempfert produces Tony Sheridan's single "My Bonnie"/"The Saints" with The Beatles backing him.

July 3—The Beatles return to Liverpool and local gigs.

July 6—first edition of *Mersey Beat*, founded by Bill Harry, who attended Liverpool College of Art with John. It is said that Brian Epstein first came across the band in its pages.

October 1–14—John and Paul holiday in Paris.

November 9—Brian Epstein and his assistant Alistair Taylor see The Beatles for the first time, at the Cavern.

December 3—first meeting between Epstein and the band. They meet again on the 6th and 10th.

December 13—Epstein invites Decca A&R man Mike Smith to the Cavern to see the band.

> 66 My contribution to Paul's songs was always to add a little bluesy edge to them... He provided a lightness, an optimism, while I would always go for sadness, the discord, the bluesy notes. 99
>
> *John Lennon*

▶ John, Paul, and Pete Best performing at the Cavern.

John Winston Lennon
October 9, 1940–December 8, 1980

John was born during wartime at the Liverpool Maternity Hospital on October 9, 1940. He was raised mostly by his mother Julia at the family home at 9 Newcastle Road, Liverpool in the suburb of Penny Lane, because his father Alfred was usually away serving in the Merchant Navy. Julia loved singing and sparked John's first interest in music.

One day in February 1944, Alfred went awol (absent without leave) and the money stopped soon after. By the time he returned six months later, Julia was pregnant with another man's child and did not want Alfred back. Julia's older, responsible sister, Mimi Smith, worried about young John, fearing that he was not properly looked after and reported Julia twice to the Social Services. In annoyance and frustration Julia then handed John's permanent care to Aunt Mimi when he was four and a half.

Aged five John was forced to choose between his father, who wanted to take him to New Zealand, and his mother. He chose his father but ran crying after his mother: he did not have contact with his father for 20 years. John later said that he soon forgot about his father altogether as he played no part in his life. Instead John lived in a semi-detached house in the desirable Liverpool suburb of Woolton, at Mendips, 251 Menlove Avenue, with Aunt Mimi and Uncle George, a dairyman. He got on well with them both and when George died, John was upset and disturbed.

◄ John with his mother Julia photographed by his cousin, Stanley Parkes.

► John, c. 1961 in Liverpool.

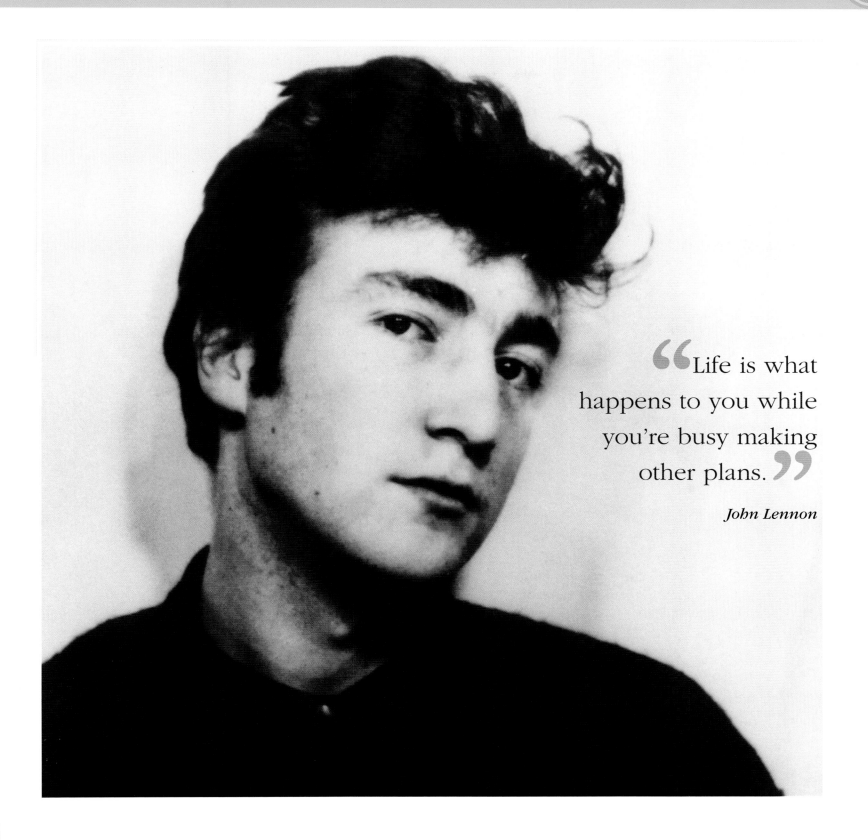

"Life is what happens to you while you're busy making other plans."

John Lennon

◄ Classic image of John posed in a doorway in Hamburg. One of the images in this sequence was used for the cover of his *Rock'n'Roll* album in 1975.

Home life changed, too, as Mimi had to take in students to help pay the bills. His mother Julia was a frequent visitor, and when he was eleven John was allowed to visit her by himself, —she lived at 1 Blomfield Road, Liverpool. She had long red hair and played the ukulele. She introduced John to modern music, especially rock'n'roll, and played him the latest records, particularly Elvis, and taught him to play the banjo.

As a teenager John admitted that he was a troublemaker, regarded as bad company by his friends' parents, and that he was probably jealous of their stable family backgrounds. He said, "I was aggressive because I wanted to be popular. I wanted to be the leader. It seemed more attractive than just being one of the toffees. I wanted everyone to do what I wanted them to do, to laugh at my jokes and let me be the boss." Nevertheless he was bright enough to pass

his Eleven-Plus and gain entry to Quarry Bank High School, but he was soon as disruptive there as before and quickly marked out as a waster.

John was always convinced that he would become a famous musician. In 1956 to encourage his optimism, his mother lent him the money to buy a cheap mail order acoustic guitar, a £5 10s Gallotone Champion, but it had to be kept well away from Aunt Mimi who disapproved of anything to do with rock'n'roll. That September John, aged 15, started his first band, The Quarrymen, named after the Quarry Bank High School. Starting out as a skiffle band they soon developed a rock'n'roll edge.

On July 6, 1957, The Quarrymen played at the St. Peter's Church garden fête where a youthful Paul McCartney watched them play. After showing off his prowess with a guitar, he was later asked if he would like to join the band. It was the first meeting of one of the very greatest song-writing partnerships.

On July 15, 1958, after visiting Mimi's house (John wasn't at home), Julia was killed by a drunk driver (an off-duty policeman) while she was standing at the bus stop waiting to go home. John was 17 years old and devastated. He subsequently failed all his exams and was only accepted by Liverpool College of Art after Mimi and his headmaster pleaded his case. By then he wore long drape coats, drainpipe trousers, grew long sideburns, and wore a quiff. He stayed for five years supposedly studying commercial art but also meeting Cynthia Powell, his future wife and a definite step up the social ladder, and Stuart Sutcliffe, a future Beatle.

At art school, which John described as "mainly one long drinking session," he was increasingly destructive and sometimes a little violent. As he grew older he listened less and less to Mimi and started to dress and behave as he wanted. He was very short-sighted but too vain to wear glasses until he saw that Buddy Holly wore them too; then he would wear them sometimes.

John had become a feckless, angry teddy boy and was excluded from one class after another for bad behavior until he was thrown out completely before the final year. Paul and George had become his fast friends and they spent a great deal of time together just hanging around waiting for something to happen. He eventually moved out of Mimi's house to a dirty barely furnished flat shared with about seven others (including Stuart Sutcliffe) in Gambier Terrace where he stayed for about four months before moving to Hamburg and the beginning of the rest of his life.

> "I definitely did look up to John. We all looked up to John. He was older and he was very much the leader; he was the quickest wit and the smartest."
>
> *Paul McCartney*

► A 1958 Rickenbacker 325 guitar with Bigsby vibrato, used as John's main guitar 1960–64.

19

Paul McCartney
18 June 1942–

> **"I knew the words to 25 rock songs, so I got in the group. 'Long Tall Sally' and 'Tutti-Frutti,' that got me in. That was my audition."**
>
> *Paul McCartney*

◄ Paul at the Cavern.

▼ Paul and his brother Mike in 1948.

James Paul McCartney was born in Liverpool, at Walton Hospital, to Mary, a midwife, and Jim (James) McCartney, a musician. Eighteen months later his brother Michael was born. Due to the demands of his mother's job the family moved around the suburbs of Liverpool quite frequently, but Paul remembers a very happy and secure childhood surrounded by family, lots of relatives and friends. He and his friends played around the bomb-sites of Liverpool, especially around the docks, which he particularly loved.

At the age of five he was sent to Stockton Wood Road Primary School, then in due course on to Joseph Williams Junior School where he passed his Eleven-Plus and gained admission to the Liverpool Institute in 1953. The following year he met George on the bus

home and they quickly became friends. In 1955 the McCartney family moved house to 20 Forthlin Road, Allerton, but tragedy struck the following year in October when Mary suffered an embolism following a mastectomy for breast cancer. He was only told the cause of his mother's death years later, but at the time the early death of their respective mothers became a strong bond between Paul and John. Along with his father and brother, Paul had to learn to do his share of the household chores, including cooking.

Both Paul's father and grandfather were musical: the former played trumpet and piano, grandfather the tuba. Encouraged by his father, Paul took music lessons for four or five weeks but gave them up when the lady started setting homework. His father was self-taught, and as he preferred to learn by ear he never learnt to read music. The McCartneys had an upright piano in their front room that his father played whenever he had the slightest opportunity (Paul still owns the instrument). Here Paul learned to play; he wrote his second song "When I'm Sixty-Four" there.

However, Paul's first instrument was the trumpet, bought by his father for his birthday. When he realized that he couldn't sing and play at the same time, he

▲ Paul McCartney.
◀ Pete Best, Paul (at piano), George, John, Stu Sutcliffe at the Top Ten Club.

asked his father if he could swap it for a guitar. His father agreed and Paul bought a £15 Framus Zenith acoustic guitar (which he still has). He soon graduated to American rhythm and blues music.

Paul had a problem: he was left-handed and most guitars were for right-handers, and it was not until he saw a photo of Slim Whitman playing with a right-handed guitar strung the opposite way ie, upside down, that he saw how to overcome it.

On July 6, 1957, aged only fifteen, Paul went to the St. Peter's Church Hall Fête in Woolton where he watched The Quarrymen play. After the gig he wandered over and was introduced to John Lennon, they talked music for a time and Paul had a little drink of beer so as to fit in with the more raucous rocker. He watched them again in the evening and even played a little piano and sang for them. The Quarrymen were all impressed at the songs he could play and the fact that he knew all the words as well. A few days later Paul bumped into their mutual friend and band member Pete Shotton, and through him he

> "None of us wanted to be the bass player. In our minds he was the fat guy who always played at the back."
>
> *Paul McCartney*

was invited to join The Quarrymen. Soon Paul joined the group and quickly became friends with John, but he made a mess of his solo at their first gig on Broadway in Liverpool. Nevertheless he was forgiven and the rest is history.

▲ A 1963 Hofner Model 500/1 violin bass owned by Paul.

George Harrison
February 25, 1943–November 29, 2001

George was born on February 25, 1943, in Liverpool, the fourth child of Louise, a shop assistant, and Harold Harrison, a bus conductor and sometime ship steward. He was born in their small bathroom-less, two-up two-down terrace home at 12 Arnold Grove, Wavertree, Liverpool, where the family lived until he was six. After waiting for years the Harrisons were moved into a newly built council house at 25 Upton Green, Speke. It had the luxury of an inside bathroom. George had a happy family with two older brothers, Pete and Harry, and a much older sister, and plenty of relatives nearby. At home he heard music from a wide selection of sources, but especially music hall songs, Irish music, and a wide variety of American music and singers.

George attended Dovedale Infants and then Dovedale Primary School a few years behind John, but they were unaware of each other as John was three years older. Although he didn't particularly like school, except for the football, George was a clever boy and passed his Eleven-Plus exams and won a place at the best school in Liverpool—the Liverpool Institute High School for Boys—and went there between 1954 and 1959.

> ❝I had no ambition when I was a kid other than to play guitar and get in a rock 'n' roll band.❞
>
> *George Harrison*

◀ The guitar George learnt to play on sold at auction in 2003 for $470,000. He bought the "Beginner's Guitar" made in Holland by Egmond and distributed by Rosetti, from schoolmate Raymond Hughes.

▶ Portrait of George on stage at the Top Ten Club in Hamburg, April 1961.

When he was about thirteen he overheard Elvis Presley singing "Heartbreak Hotel" coming from a nearby house. The sound struck him like a thunderbolt and changed his life. From then on he said that he completely lost interest in school and wanted to devote himself to music. He had fallen in love with guitar music and desperately wanted to own an instrument himself.

George was prone to sore throats and tonsillitis and one year when he was around thirteen, it turned into nephritis, an infection of the kidneys, and he had to go into Alder Hey Hospital for six weeks. While there George decided that he had to have a guitar. He had heard that an old acquaintance wanted to sell his for £3 10s, a lot of money for a penniless boy, but his mum found it for him and he bought the guitar: a Dutch Egmond flat top acoustic. It soon fell apart, but brother Pete fixed it for him. Also his father arranged for an old friend of his, Len Houghton, to give George guitar lessons on Thursday evenings. Len taught him to play and introduced George to popular songs from the

◄ George Harrison playing a Futurama guitar at the Top Ten Club. Paul is in the background.

1920s and 1930s as well as some of the Jazz greats like Django Reinhardt.

Inspired by the music, George formed a skiffle group with his brother Pete and school friend Arthur Kelly (who went on to become a successful TV actor) at the Institute. They called themselves the Rebels. They only got to play one gig, at the local British Legion Club.

Paul was around nine months older and one year ahead of George at school. He used to live a bus stop away from him when they both lived in Speke. They got to know each other on the bus and became friends when they discovered a mutual passion for music, particularly Elvis, Buddy Holly, and Little Richard. Totally guitar-obsessed, George lived and breathed guitar music, learning as much as he could from wherever he could find it. His schoolwork suffered but he and Paul hung out together at school and remained firm friends even after Paul's family moved a 20-minute bike ride away.

When Paul joined The Quarrymen, he lobbied heavily with the others to bring in George as lead guitar. They agreed to audition him, but the first time around John rejected him, not because he couldn't play, but because at 14 he was so much younger (and looked it): John was 17 and Paul 15. Paul, however, was determined that George should join them so he arranged another audition, this time on the top deck of an empty bus. George played "Raunchy" and blew them all away. He was in the band. At that time John was still playing banjo chords and only had four strings on his guitar until George told him that he should have six and taught him some real chords.

After George left school he wasn't interested in getting a job or returning for more schooling. His father wanted him to become an electrician but he failed to pass the exam to get a job with Liverpool Corporation. Then, more by accident than design, he got a job as an apprentice electrician: his father was happy, but all the while he was determined in his head to become a musician, he just didn't know how.

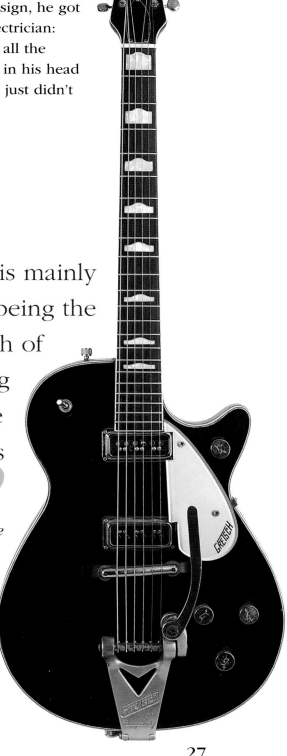

> "George is mainly famous for being the quiet one, which of course is a big joke because he never stops talking."
>
> *Eric Idle*

▶ A 1957 Gretsch Duo Jet fitted with a Bigsby vibrato owned by George Harrison.

27

The Quarrymen

Mostly pupils at Quarry Bank High School, The Quarrymen were formed by John Lennon, Eric Griffiths, and a few friends in 1956 to play skiffle, but they soon turned into a rock'n'roll band.

John's mother Julia taught John to play the banjo, and then taught him and Eric a few chords and songs (Eric could already play the banjo). The pair also took formal guitar lessons, but John found the theory boring and soon gave up.

Eric and John practiced together at their respective homes where they learnt a number of popular songs. In summer 1956 they started their own skiffle group, briefly calling themselves The Blackjacks, before settling on The Quarrymen. The initial members were John, Eric, Pete Shotton (on washboard, he soon left the band), Bill Smith (bass—tea chest), and Rod Davis (banjo). Smith rarely turned up for rehearsals, so was rapidly replaced by Len Garry (on the tea chest). They soon found a drummer with his own drums in Colin Hanton. Their manager was another friend: Nigel Walley. When they felt confident enough to play in public, John designed a series of fliers which Nigel sent around to local places of entertainment.

They played covers of popular rock'n'roll songs locally at any gig they could get: school dances, parties, and so on. After a successful gig at the Lee Park Golf Club, The Quarrymen were asked to fill the interlude spot—playing skiffle not rock'n'roll—between two jazz bands at The Cavern Club in Mathew Street, Liverpool.

Saturday, June 25, 1957, was the 750th anniversary of the granting of Liverpool's city charter by King John. For the celebrations, The Quarrymen played two sets from the back of a flatbed lorry at the street party in Rosebery Street. They didn't get paid but it was good experience and the photographs of the event show a young John with a Teddy Boy quiff, front and center at the microphone.

Their most significant moment came eleven days later on Saturday, July 6, when on a warm and sunny day The Quarrymen played at St. Peter's Church garden fête in Woolton. First they played on the back of a flatbed lorry as part of the float procession, then on stage in a field near the church, then a gig in the evening in the church hall for the grand dance. During the afternoon set Paul McCartney wandered along and was later introduced to John in the scout hut as he prepared for the evening. Paul played a few songs and explained to an intrigued John how he tuned his guitar.

After discussions together, John and Pete decided to invite Paul to join them. He agreed, but wanted to go on a family holiday first. At rehearsals with Paul it quickly became clear that rock'n'roll was to be their direction and on his return from holiday banjo-playing Rod decided to leave the band.

Paul played his first gig with The Quarrymen at a Conservative Party social on October 18 at the New Clubmoor Hall, Liverpool. He was so nervous that he fluffed most of his cues.

George first saw The Quarrymen perform on February 6, 1958, at Wilson Hall and auditioned to join them the following month. As he was only 14, John said no. But Paul was determined that George join them and managed to get John and George onto the top deck of a bus together, where George auditioned again. After more petitioning John finally relented and allowed George into the band as lead guitar: he had just turned 15. Eric had not been told and left soon after. Len also left after a time as he became severely ill with tuberculous meningitis.

Soon John, Paul, and George were hanging out together despite their age differences, because they shared similar tastes in music. Sometimes Paul would bunk off school and John would miss college and they'd meet at Paul's house where they could practice their guitars. They started to write songs together and Paul wrote them down in an exercise book. He annotated each song with "Another Lennon/McCartney original". Two of their early songs were "I Saw Her Standing There" and "Love Me Do." One by one the others left The Quarrymen until it was just the hardcore three: John, Paul, and George. They even played The Cavern Club once but were too rock'n'roll for the clientele.

They were heavily influenced by American rhythm and blues, in particular Chuck Berry and Buddy Holly. Their first recording was made on July 12, 1958, in a very basic studio. The Quarrymen were John, Paul, George, Colin Hanton and "Duff" Lowe. They played "That'll Be The Day," with John singing on one side and "In Spite Of All The Danger" (written by Paul and George) sung by Paul and John with George playing lead guitar on the other. The cost was 17s 6d (86.5p). That got them one vinyl 78rpm disc. They agreed that they would each have it for a week. It finally ended up with Duff who kept it for 23 years and then sold it back to Paul for considerably more than it originally cost.

On July 15, 1958, Julia Lennon was knocked down and killed. John was devastated and for a time

▲ The Quarrymen's first concert at the Casbah Coffee Club on August 29, 1959.

lost interest in the music. However, The Quarrymen continued with the odd gig including the wedding reception of George's brother Harry, and a regular alternate Friday night slot at Liverpool Art School. Once, following a poor gig and a drunken argument with Paul, Colin left never to be seen again.

After many ups and downs, The Quarrymen secured a residency at the Casbah Coffee Club in Liverpool, but they soon fell out with the owner (Mona Best) and left. After playing around the Liverpool area, with different names and lineups, John invited his art school friend Stuart Sutcliffe to join. He bought an expensive Höfner 500/5 bass: only problem was, he wasn't (according to Paul) very good at playing it. They didn't mind though, it looked great on stage. Soon after, they changed their name to the Silver Beetles and in May 1960 toured Scotland under that name. They became The Beatles when they got the gigs in Hamburg, Germany.

Hamburg

Hamburg, like Liverpool, was a vibrant city and port where anything and everything was available for people who wanted to experience life. The city had a well-deserved reputation for vice and debauchery and all the temptations of a thriving sea port. The band visited Hamburg five times over the course of two and a half years and played a total of 281 concerts there.

The first time they went to Germany there were five Beatles—John, Paul, George, Stuart Sutcliffe, and Pete Best—it was 1960 and George was only 17 years old. For their first trip ten people, including The Beatles, squeezed into their booking agent Allan William's Austin Minivan. He drove them to the ferry at Harwich that crossed to the Hook of Holland. After docking in Germany on August 16, 1960, they then drove to Hamburg. They had been contracted for a season (although Williams hoped to replace them with a better band) to follow in the footsteps of other British bands. The group was paid £100 a week, much better than they were getting in Liverpool. But at that time they had no drummer and so quickly drafted in Pete

> 66 Hamburg totally wrecked us. I remember getting home to England and my dad thought I was half-dead. I looked like a skeleton. I hadn't noticed the change, I'd been having such a ball! 99
>
> *Paul McCartney*

◄ The Indra Club on Grosse Freiheit in the St. Pauli district of Hamburg, Germany.

Best a couple of days before they left—in fact he was the only drummer they could find who agreed to go to Hamburg.

Their first gig was on August 17, 1960, at the Indra Club, at 64 Grosse Freiheit, a seedy strip club cum music venue on the fringes of the Reeperbahn red-light area in the St. Pauli district. Their digs were behind the screen of the Bambi Kino cinema and comprised a couple of bunk beds in unheated and squalid storage rooms next to the smelly toilets. But they were learning their trade, getting tighter and better, playing to a mixed audience of late night revelers and tourists. Their sets were from 8:30 to 9:30, 10 to 11, 11:30 to 12:30, and then from 1 to 2am, seven days a week.

The club was so noisy it was closed down and The Beatles moved to playing at the larger and much more popular Kaiserkeller (owned by the same people), starting there on October 4, 1960. Their schedule was just as grueling as before and the living conditions not much better—a back room in the Kaiserkeller. But now they were actively encouraged to put on a show, so they started to play around a lot more on stage, much to the delight of the audience. Within days they were joined by the far more professional Rory Storm and the Hurricanes for whom Ringo Starr drummed—they were also getting better paid. The Beatles were warned they would have to become more professional so as not to suffer by comparison. The Beatles and the Hurricanes alternated each doing a 90-minute set.

It was here that they met graphic artist Klaus Voormann (who would later design the cover for *Revolver* and play in the Plastic Ono Band) his girlfriend Astrid Kirchherr and Jürgen Vollmer. They were all knocked out by The Beatles and became their biggest fans and then friends. Kirchherr took photos

▲ Poster for the Kaiserkeller advertising Rory Storm & The Hurricanes and The Beatles, October/November 1960.

of them in the nearby Der Dom fairground which impressed them. She started dating Stuart and by November 1960 they were engaged.

The audience at the Kaiserkeller was rowdy and it was not unusual for beer bottles and fists to fly. They were all pleased with their progress. They were starting to attract their own audience—even the other groups would come and watch them perform.

▲John, Paul, and George onstage in Hamburg, April 1961.

Having worked to get an audience The Beatles were poached by the Top Ten Club with the offer of better money, somewhat better sleeping quarters, and a better PA. The owner of the Kaiserseller was furious and as a result George was reported for being under age and deported on November 30, 1960. Then on December 4, 1960, Paul and Pete were deported on a ridiculous charge of attempted arson. John's work permit was revoked a few days later. All their equipment was left behind. Stuart stayed in Hamburg to be with Astrid and returned later in January.

They returned to Hamburg in 1961 when their immigration problems were sorted out, for a residency at the Top Ten Club between April 1 and July 1. This time the accommodation was in a room above the club, still bunk beds and basic, but better than before. Stuart soon decided that the life wasn't for him and left to be with Astrid and resume his art studies. This meant that Paul had to move to playing bass guitar, something he didn't want to do. Now with a bit more money they bought new instruments and new stage clothes—black leather jackets, jeans, and cowboy boots.

Their workload was not easy: it was typical to start at 7pm and play on through to around 7am. An extreme example was in 1961 when they played for 98 nights in succession at the Top Ten Club with only short breaks during each session. To keep going they learnt to take a steady medication of uppers, specifically morphine-based Preludin (Prellies)—supposedly prescription only— given to them by the club management, the waiters, and Astrid. Taken with beer this would keep them going for hours. They certainly paid their dues. They spent most of their little free time drinking and smoking in the Reeperbahn at the Kaiserkeller and the Gretel & Alfons kneipe (pub).

The following year The Beatles were booked for the opening of the Star Club, a cinema-style

> "I grew up in Hamburg, not Liverpool."
>
> *John Lennon*

venue with capacity for 2,000 people and a great sound system. They flew over to Hamburg for the opening gig on April 13 to be met on arrival by Astrid Kirchherr who told them about Stuart's death. This residency lasted until May 31, 1962.

They were booked again by the Star Club for November 1–14, 1962. During this period Ringo became their drummer, but only on condition that they improve themselves because he didn't want to play with amateurs. For the first time they were able to afford the comfort of a hotel and a room each. They were booked again for December 18–31, 1962. Within a few weeks of their final gig they were top of the charts with their second single "Please Please Me."

▲ Self portrait by Jürgen Vollmer in 1962.

◀ Stu Sutcliffe and John at the Top Ten Club.

The Other Beatles

Pete Best
24 November 1941–

◄ Pete Best in Hamburg.

Pete was born in Madras (now Chennai) in India on November 24, 1941, at which time he was called Randolph Peter. His father, Donald Scanland, died during World War II and his mother Mona later met and married Liverpudlian Johnny Best. They left India on the last troopship in 1945 and moved to Liverpool.

Pete played drums in groups around Liverpool and had been playing in The Black Jacks until they broke up. His mother ran the Casbah Coffee Club in Hayman's Green where The Quarrymen occasionally played and Pete sometimes sat in on drums. Then in autumn 1960 he was asked by Paul to audition for The Beatles. They had just secured a residency to play for two months in Hamburg but had no drummer. The Beatles knew he was a good-looking guy

> "We were cowards when we sacked him. We made Brian do it. "
>
> *John Lennon*

who could really drive a beat and attract the girls. He auditioned in Allan William's Jacaranda club, agreed to £15 a week, and was in the minivan with the others heading for Hamburg the next day. The alternative was going to teacher-training college. In fact no other drummer was willing to go to Hamburg, but Pete wasn't told at the time in case he asked for more money. It also turned out that he was the only member of the group who had a smattering of German so he became the group's translator.

The gigs in Hamburg were long and demanding but often fun: they lived hard and played hard and all improved immensely with the long hours of gigging. Pete's drumming got louder and more insistent as Paul frequently told him to "crank it up" and play as loud and hard as possible. They left the Kaiserkeller acrimoniously: Paul and Pete were maliciously accused of arson, locked up in prison for three hours, and then deported on December 4, 1960. Forced to leave Germany without their equipment, they didn't bother to contact each other, but Pete and mother Mona spent ages phoning Hamburg to try to recover their gear. After this Mona became their booker and took care of much of The Beatles' administration. She got them their first sets at the Cavern Club.

They returned to Hamburg and long hours of gigging in April 1961. At the end of the year Brian Epstein became their manager, taking over much of Mona's role. Brian got them an audition at Decca Records on New Year's Day, 1962, and later at Parlophone with George Martin during which they recorded four songs. Martin and his engineers felt that Pete was not precise enough for a recording and instead used a session drummer.

After the first audition for Parlophone, George Martin asked Paul, John, and George whether they would consider changing Pete because he couldn't keep time the way he thought necessary. They were horrified at the thought but also afraid that if they refused they would also lose this slim chance of success. George Martin later said he only wanted the other drummer for recording and hadn't meant that Pete be dropped from the band for live shows.

The other Beatles made the pragmatic decision that Pete had to go but asked Brian Epstein to actually dismiss him. Brian himself was unwilling to break up the group and agonized about it. Finally, he called Pete into his office on August 16, 1962, and gave him the bad news. The reasons behind his sacking are disputed: some reports suggest that Pete was something of a loner and did not really hang around with the other three Beatles. He also never agreed to take the Preludin drugs that kept them awake for their long playing sessions. Other analysts said that he was too limited as a drummer and would have held the group back musically had he stayed. All the other Beatles later went on record to say that they regretted the manner of his dismissal.

Pete had been with The Beatles two years and four days. He was absolutely furious at his dismissal as was his best friend Neil Aspinall, the band's PA cum roadie. Neil was also determined to walk away but Pete persuaded him to stay. The news first became public when reported on the front page of *Mersey Beat* on August 23 and many of The Beatles' fans were very upset. The band were heckled and booed at a number of gigs—"Pete Best forever, Ringo never!"—for the next few weeks and George was even headbutted outside The Cavern leaving him with a black eye.

Back in London George Martin was shocked at the news of the sacking as he considered Pete to be the biggest selling point of the band as far as female fans were concerned. Within a few weeks he was replaced by Ringo Starr who was already well known to the band: he had even sat in for Pete on a number of occasions.

Brian Epstein tried to build another band around Pete Best but although they signed to Decca they were not a success.

The Other Beatles

Stu Sutcliffe June 23, 1940–April 10, 1962

Stuart Ferguson Victor Sutcliffe was born in Edinburgh but moved with his family to Liverpool when he was three. After schooling in Liverpool he attended Liverpool College of Art where he met and quickly became fast friends with John. However, to earn enough to live he also worked as a bin man for Liverpool Corporation.

Stuart showed real promise as an artist and was regarded at the college as one to watch. He was principally an Abstract Expressionist and some of his works hang in Liverpool art galleries. He used his talent to help other students, including John, to improve their artistic techniques. The two became close (so much so that Paul later admitted to being a bit jealous). In 1960 John moved into Stuart's shared flat in Gambier Terrace: it was squalid with only few pieces of tatty furniture and mattresses on the floor for beds.

> **"**I looked up to Stu, I depended on him to tell me the truth … Stu would tell me if something was good, and I'd believe him.**"**
>
> *John Lennon*

◀ ▶ Stu Sutcliffe played bass before dying of a brain tumor in 1962.

Stuart could play the bugle, a little piano, and guitar, and he could sing—skills the Silver Beatles could use, so John and Paul urged him to join their group and buy a Höfner President 500/5 bass guitar (on hire purchase). In fact none of the other three wanted to play bass, so it was the obvious vacancy. He officially joined in May 1960 and they used the flat as a rehearsal room; additionally Stuart took on the role of looking for gigs until Allan Williams took over.

Stuart was good looking and the girls took particular notice of him in his tight trousers and dark glasses. He certainly attracted more female attention than the others, so first Paul and then John seemed to grow jealous of his popularity and their personal relationships started to suffer. When the Beatles got to Hamburg he attracted the attention of Astrid Kirchherr: the appeal was mutual and they soon paired up. They got engaged in November 1960 and moved into the Kirchherr family home.

In July 1961 Stuart decided that he had enough of The Beatles and quit the group. He had learnt that Eduardo Paolozzi was going to become a lecturer at Hamburg Art College and as he was something of a hero to him, he wanted to make the most of the opportunity. He had also decided that he wanted to spend more time with Astrid and to devote himself to art instead of music. The others weren't particularly surprised but it left them without a bass player. John and George refused flat out to play bass, but Paul said he would give it a go. Accordingly Stuart lent Paul his Höfner President until he had enough money to buy his own—provided he didn't re-string it; Paul had to play it upside down to comply. Stuart then took up a postgraduate scholarship at Hamburg College of Art where he studied under the tutelage of Paolozzi who considered him to be one of his best students.

Around the same time Stuart started to suffer from debilitating headaches and became extremely sensitive to light. Sometimes he even experienced temporary blindness. One day he collapsed in art class in Hamburg but the doctors who examined him were unable to find an explanation. He was advised to return to England but chose not to. His headaches got worse until on April 10, 1962, he collapsed and was taken by ambulance to hospital (with Astrid accompanying him) but he died before he could get there. The autopsy discovered an aneurysm in the right ventricle of his brain causing a fatal hemorrhage. It was probably caused by an earlier head injury but it might also have been genetic. His mother flew to Hamburg and took his body back to Liverpool. His funeral was held in Liverpool. Of The Beatles, John, in particular, was devastated. Stuart Sutcliffe is included on the extreme left in the montage on the *Sgt. Pepper* album.

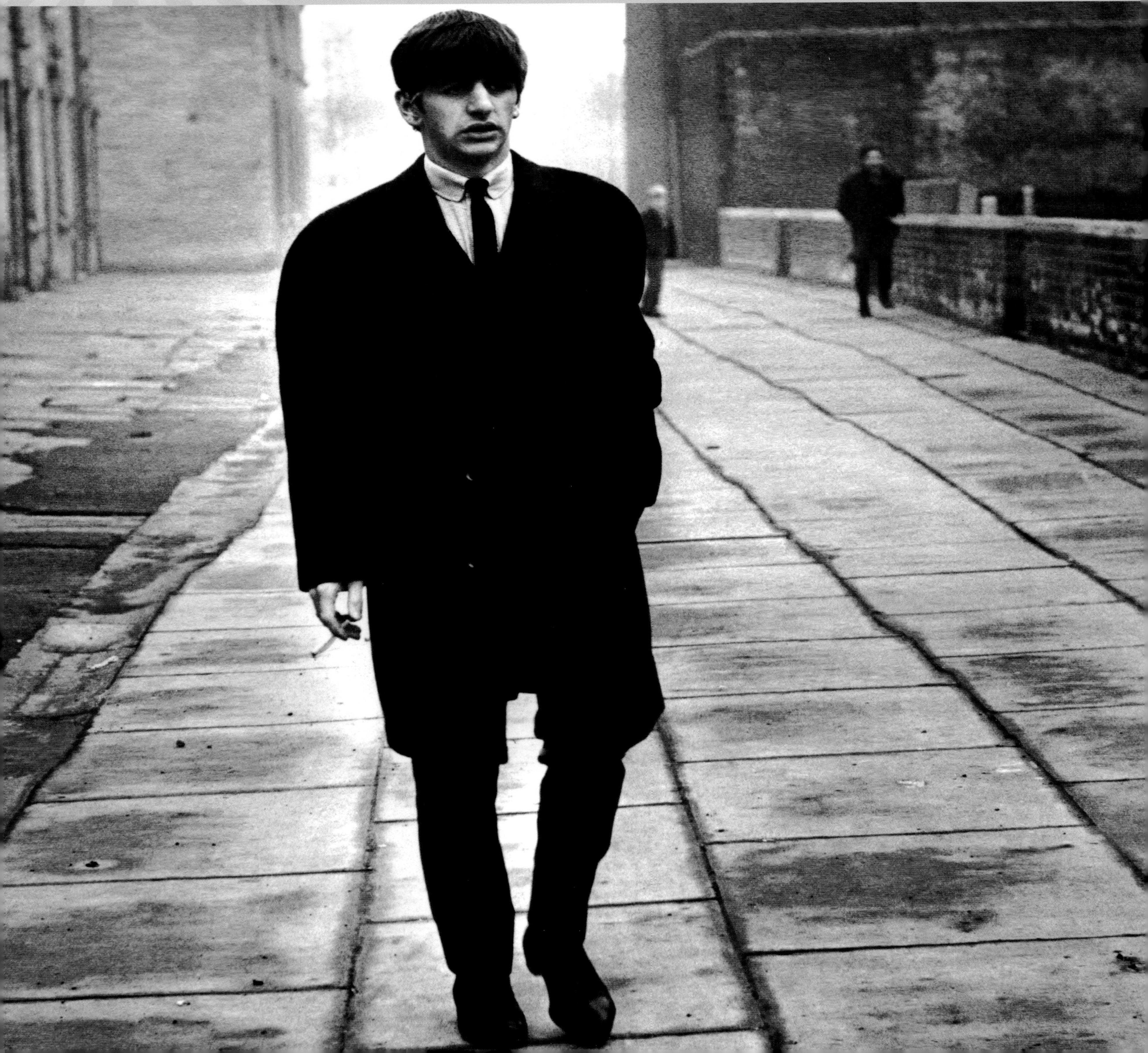

ON THE WAY TO THE TOP

1962-63

> "Most of the time we wrote together. We'd go and lock ourselves away and say, 'OK, what have we got?' . . . by the end of three or four hours we nearly always had it cracked! I can't remember coming away from one of those sessions not having finished a song."
>
> *Paul McCartney*

◀ Ringo leaving the family home in Admiral Grove on December 7, 1963, on his way to the Empire Theatre to film a special edition of *Juke Box Jury*.

Timeline

1962

January 1—the Decca audition at Decca Records, 165 Broadhurst Gardens, London. They record fifteen songs but in the end (around February 10) Dick Rowe says, "Go back to Liverpool, Mr. Epstein. Groups with guitars are out."

January 4—the band is voted Liverpool's top group in *Mersey Beat*.

January 5—Tony Sheridan and the Beatles "My Bonnie"/"The Saints" single released in the UK.

January 24—The Beatles sign with Brian Epstein and NEMS (North End Music Store). He gets 25 percent of the takings.

February 12—first BBC audition.

March 7—The Beatles record the first of 52 BBC radio shows they will do between March 1962 and May 1965. Only two of the three songs recorded are broadcast on *Teenagers' Turn – Here We Go* the following day. Other *Teenagers' Turn* sessions air on June 15 and October 26, with three more programs in 1963.

April 10—Stuart Sutcliffe dies of a brain hemorrhage in Hamburg aged 21.

April 13–May 31—The Beatles

▲ The man who turned down The Beatles: Decca Records producer and A&R man Dick Rowe (1921–86), c.1965.

return to Hamburg, playing at the Star Club.

May 9—Brian Epstein meets George Martin and signs a contract with Parlophone (owned by EMI) ... if they pass the audition.

June 6—A few days after their return from Hamburg, The Beatles audition at Abbey Road and George Martin signs them up, although there are questions about Pete Best's drumming.

August 15—Pete Best plays his last gig with the band: the next day he is sacked and Ringo is taken on.

August 18—Ringo's first gig with The Beatles, although he had sat in for Pete Best a couple of times in the past.

August 22—The Beatles' first TV session is recorded by Granada at the Cavern. It won't air until November 6's *Scene at 6:30*. It shows the band performing "Some Other Guy" and is the earliest live footage of the "Fab Four" lineup. They will appear nine times on this daily news show, the last on October 16, 1964.

August 23—John marries Cynthia Powell at Mount Pleasant Register Office, Liverpool. Present are George Harrison, Paul McCartney, Brian Epstein, and Tony Powell.

September 4—The Beatles' first recording session since signing to EMI. At Abbey Road they record "Love Me Do" and "How Do You Do It."

September 11—another recording session at Abbey Road working on "Love Me Do," "P.S. I Love You," and "Please Please Me" with session drummer, Andy White.

October 1—The Beatles sign a five-year contract with Brian

Epstein, he still gets 25 percent of their earnings.

October 5—The Beatles' first solo UK single release: "Love Me Do"/"P.S. I Love You."

October 8—The Beatles record an interview for Radio Luxembourg (broadcast on October 12).

October 13—"Love Me Do" enters the UK singles chart: it will spend eighteen weeks in the charts.

October 17—The Beatles' second TV recording session provides their first national TV appearance ... live

▼The Star Club opened April 13, 1962, with The Beatles starting the first of seven weeks of gigs.

on Granada's *People and Places*. They will appear on the show four times.

November 1–14—contractual obligations take the band back to Hamburg where they play at the Star Club. Little Richard is also there and the band meets his young African-American keyboard player, Billy Preston.

November 16—back in London the band records for Radio Luxembourg's *The Friday Spectacular*, which airs on November 23.

November 26—the band records again at Abbey Road: "Please Please Me," "Ask Me Why," and "Tip of My Tongue."

December 18–30—The Beatles' final Hamburg residency.

December 27—"Love Me Do" reaches its highest spot on the UK charts—No.17.

1963

January 2–8—The Beatles go on a short tour of Scotland. It ends with a live performance of "Please Please Me" on Scottish TV's

▲(L–R) John, Ringo, Paul, and George onstage during their final residency at the Star Club.

Roundup.

January 11—UK single released: "Please Please Me"/"Ask Me Why." Unhappy with the publicity for the first single, Epstein recruits Dick James Music as publisher and Tony Barrow to help with publicity.

January 13—The Beatles record "Please Please Me" for ABC TV's *Thank Your Lucky Stars* which airs on January 19. Other TV publicity for the single includes *People and Places* live on the 16th, and another *Thank Your Lucky Stars* which airs on February 23.

January 16—The Beatles record *Please Please Me* for *Teenagers' Turn – Here We Go*.

▲ With Gene Vincent at the Star Club in April–May 1962.

Other radio promotion for the new single includes another Radio Luxembourg The Friday Spectacular, which airs on the 25th, and three BBC shows: *Pop Inn* (22nd), *Saturday Club* (26th), and *The Talent Spot* (29th). The band will appear ten times on *Saturday Club* over the years. Helped by the publicity, "Please Please Me" enters the UK singles chart on January 19.

January 20—Mal Evans becomes a road manager, splitting the functions with Neil Aspinall. After touring ends in 1966, they will stay on as general factotums.

February 2—start of the band's first UK tour, headlined by Helen Shapiro, with fourteen dates, the first of which is at Bradford's Gaumont Cinema. During the

tour, on the 23rd, "Please Please Me" makes No.1 on the *NME* and *Melody Maker* charts and No.2 on the *Record Retailer* chart.

February 11—three long sessions at Abbey Road (10:00–13:00; 14:30–18:00; 19:30–22:45) is all it takes to record The Beatles' first album, *Please Please Me*.

February 20—Geoff Emerick's first work with The Beatles. He's second engineer on the album overdubs. He will go on to become their engineer from *Revolver* onward.

February 25—US release of "Please Please Me"/"Ask Me Why" on Vee Jay records after Capitol rejects it.

March 3—Last date of the Helen Shapiro tour at the Gaumont

▼ A poster for "The Beatles Show" at The Rialto Ballroom, Liverpool, September 6, 1962.

Cinema in Hanley, Staffordshire.

March 5—The Beatles record "From Me To You" at Abbey Road.

March 9–31—the second tour of the year, this one with Tommy Roe and Chris Montez headlining ... but crowd response and the chart

> "I first saw the Beatles in a club in Hamburg. They were very scruffy characters — but they had a beat in their music which I liked...I got into a lot of trouble over it. Everyone said they were too rough, too untidy. But I liked them. I put them on again and again."
>
> *Johnny Hamp*
> *(People and Places producer)*

LEACH ENTERTAINMENT
★ ★ ★ PRESENT ★ ★ ★
OPERATION BIG BEAT 5
TOWER BALLROOM
NEW BRIGHTON
FRI., SEPT. 14 - 1962
7:30 P. M. TO 1:00 A. M.
STARRING THE NORTH'S TOP ROCK COMBO
The
BEATLES
★
RORY STORM
With The HURRICANES
♪ GERRY ♪
& THE PACEMAKERS
BILLY KRAMER
WITH THE COASTERS
ALSO: THE 4 JAYS & THE MERSEY BEATS
TICKETS 5/ FROM - RUSHWORTHS, NEMS, CRANES
TOP HAT RECORD BAR, TOWER BALLROOM

▲Wirral gig just before the release of "Love Me Do," September 14, 1962.

success of "Please Please Me" make The Beatles the headline act.

March 22—UK release of the *Please Please Me* album. A remarkable debut, it will spend an amazing thirty weeks at No.1.

April 5—The Beatles receive their first silver disc, for the single, "Please Please Me." They receive it at EMI House, 10 Manchester Square, London, where they play a short gig for EMI staff.

April 8—John Charles Julian Lennon is born at Sefton General Hospital, Liverpool, weighing 6lb. 11oz.

April 11—UK single release "From Me To You"/"Thank You Girl." On

April 20 it enters the charts.

April 14—after recording a mime "From Me To You" for *Thank Your Lucky Stars*, The Beatles see the Rolling Stones for the first time at the Crawdaddy Club in Richmond. Afterward they go on to party at 102 Edith Grove, West Brompton, where Mick Jagger, Brian Jones, and Keith Richards live.

April 18—The Beatles play at the Royal Albert Hall in the *Swinging Sounds '63* show where Paul meets Jane Asher. Also on the bill is Del Shannon who hears them play "From Me To You." He records it soon after and it becomes the first

Lennon–McCartney song to make the US charts (although credited to McCartney–Lennon, as were all their songs before this).

April 28—The Beatles have their first holiday. Paul, George, and Ringo go to Tenerife for 12 days; John and Brian Epstein go to Spain.

May 1—Tony Barrow leaves Decca to join NEMS as The Beatles' press officer.

May 4—"From Me To You" makes No.1 on the UK singles charts: it will remain there for seven weeks.

▼Julian was born on April 8, 1963. This is John and Julian in 1966.

May 18—start of a UK tour with Roy Orbison and Gerry and the Pacemakers at the Adelphi Cinema, Slough.

May 27—Vee Jay release "From Me To You"/"Thank You Girl" in the US. Lack of promotion limits it to three weeks in the charts and a top position of No. 116.

June 4—the BBC's *Pop Goes The Beatles* airs for the first time. There will be fifteen programs in all, affording great publicity.

June 8—"My Bonnie," released by Polydor to capitalize on the band's success, spends a week on the UK singles chart at No.48.

June 9—the band's third British tour ends in Blackburn.

June 18—Paul's 21st birthday party at his aunt's home. John attacks Bob Wooler, a long-time friend, when he insinuates that John and Brian had a homosexual relationship on their recent holiday.

June 22—John records an appearance for the BBC's *Juke Box Jury*: it's broadcast on the 29th.

June 26—John and Paul finalize "She Loves You" in a hotel room in Newcastle. They will start recording

it at Abbey Road on July 1.

July 8–13—residency in the Winter Gardens, Margate.

July 12—UK release of the Twist and Shout EP ("Twist and Shout," "A Taste of Honey," "Do You Want To Know A Secret," and "There's A Place"). It will spend 64 weeks in the charts, 21 of them at No.1.

July 18—The Beatles begin recording *With The Beatles* at Abbey Road.

July 22—Vee Jay intend to release their version of the album *Please Please Me*, named *Introducing The Beatles*, but it is cancelled after a management shakeup.

July 22–27—residency at the Odeon, Weston-super-Mare.

August 1—The first issue of *The Beatles Book* goes on sale with a print run of 80,000—under a quarter of what the monthly publication will rise to by the end of the year. It runs until December 1969 (77 issues).

August 3—the last of 274 gigs the band played at the Cavern.

August 6–10—The Beatles play five dates in the Channel Islands.

August 12–17—a week-long residency at the Odeon Cinema, Llandudno, two shows a night.

August 19–24—a week-long residency at the Gaumont Cinema Bournemouth, during which

▼The band performing at the London Palladium, October 13, 1963.

> 〝'Please Please Me' was the first time they showed they could write a great song. I wasn't convinced they could do it again. 'From Me to You' changed my mind. It was a super song.〞
>
> *George Martin*

▲ Reading letters from fans.

(on the 22nd) Robert Freeman photographed them for the cover of *With The Beatles*.

August 23—release in the UK of the single "She Loves You"/"I'll Get You": it will enter the charts on **August 31** and become the band's first million seller.

August 26–31—A week-long residency at the Odeon Cinema, Southport.

September—all four Beatles move into Flat L at 57 Green Street, Mayfair, the only place in which they lived together. John moves out in November 1963 and Paul later moves into Jane Asher's family home (57 Wimpole Street, Marylebone), leaving George and Ringo in the flat.

September 6—release in the UK of EP *The Beatles' Hits* ("From Me To You," "Thank You Girl," "Please Please Me," and "Love Me Do").

It goes to No.1 and spends 43 weeks on the EP charts.

September 12—She Loves You reaches No.1 on the UK singles chart: it's there for four weeks and for two more from November 28.

September 16—John and Cynthia holiday in Paris; George goes to visit his sister in Illinois; and Paul, Jane Asher, Ringo, and Maureen go to Greece.

September 24—the final *Pop Goes The Beatles* program leads with "She Loves You." Millions of teenagers had tuned into the BBC on Thursdays at 17:50 to listen to their idols.

October 4—The Beatles' first appearance on ITV's *Ready Steady Go!*

October 5–7—The Beatles play three gigs in Scotland (Glasgow, Kirkcaldy, Dundee).

October 13—The Beatles

play four songs for their first appearance on *Sunday Night at the London Palladium* to a live audience of over fifteen million. Next day, the Press goes wild and the *Daily Mirror* coins the epithet "Beatlemania."

October 17—"I Want To Hold Your Hand" recorded at Abbey Road.

October 23—the band flies to Sweden, for their first big overseas gigs. They play six dates (Stockholm 24/26, Karlstad 25, Göterborg 27, Boras 28, Eskilstuna 29).

October 29—Brian signs a deal with United Artists that leads to the film *A Hard Day's Night*.

October 31—The Beatles fly in to London's Heathrow Airport from

Sweden. The huge number of fans and their response to the band is noted by Ed Sullivan, who is leaving for the US and leads to a booking for his TV show.

November—John, Cynthia, and Julian move to 13 Emperors Gate, Brompton, Knightsbridge and live there under the name "Hadley" until July 1964.

November 1—*The Beatles (No.1)*, an EP of songs from the album *Please Please Me*, is released in the UK. Its best chart position is No. 2.

November 1–December 13—the first gig of a 36-date autumn tour is at the Odeon Cinema, Cheltenham.

November 4—the band is the seventh act at the Royal Variety Performance broadcast by ATV on the 10th. During the gig, Lennon delivers his famous intro, "On the next number would those in the cheap seats clap their hands? The rest of you, rattle your jewelry."

November 15—*Time* magazine's "The New Madness" article is the first mainstream US journalism on the band.

November 16—before the show at Bournemouth's Winter Gardens, CBS interviews the band and later CBS, ABC, and NBC all filmed part of the concert.

▲ "I Want to Hold Your Hand" was released on Capitol Records on December 26, 1963.

November 18—*Newsweek* runs an article on Beatlemania.

November 22—*With The Beatles* is released in the UK. It becomes the first million-selling LP in Britain.

November—in the publicity for the new album, Tony Barrow coins the term "Fab Four."

November 29—the single "I Want To Hold Your Hand"/"This Boy" released in the UK with advance sales of over one million. On **December 14** it displaces "She Loves You" from No.1 and stays there for five weeks. Total UK sales are around 1.75 million.

December 1—*The New York Times* runs a three-page article on Beatlemania.

December 7—after a concert at the Empire Theatre, Liverpool the band rushes to the Odeon Cinema

> **A** midnight panic swept through the crowd at Carlisle; girls screamed, sirens wailed. Four thousand stood all night at Newcastle, faces pinched and grim in a drenching rain. Fifty bobbies were needed to fight the crush at Hull in Yorkshire. 'Beatlemania,' as Britons call the new madness, was striking everywhere ....

TIME magazine

for a special edition of the BBC's *Juke Box Jury*, where they take the four places on the jury.

December 18—the band records songs for a BBC bank holiday radio special, at that time called "Beatletime." It is broadcast as *From Us To You on Boxing Day*, December 26. It is a great success and leads to follow-ups on other bank holidays in 1964. The host for the program is Rolf Harris—and the band joins him on a version of "Tie Me Kangeroo Down, Sport."

December 24–January 11—the first Beatles Christmas Show runs for sixteen nights at the Astoria Cinema, Finsbury Park, London after previewing at the Gaumont Cinema, Bradford on December 21.

December 26—the first Capitol release of a single by the band—"I Want To Hold Your Hand"/"I Saw Her Standing There." It will sell some five million copies in the US, reaching No.1 on February 1.

▶ The Beatles rehearse for *The Morcambe and Wise Show*, December 2, 1963.

Richard Starkey

aka Ringo Starr July 7, 1940–

Ringo Starr was born during wartime at home at 9 Madryn Street, Dingle, Liverpool. Soon after, Liverpool suffered heavy enemy bombing. Their neighborhood was very badly damaged and his family had to shelter in the coal cellar. His parents, Elsie and Richard Starkey (a cake baker), named him Richard. They split up when he was three. After his father left, Richard only met him a few times and never bonded

▼ Teddy boy Ringo circa 1959.

with him. His mother was forced to do a variety of jobs, whatever she could get—working in shops, as a barmaid, or cleaning—to put food on the table and keep a roof over their head. They had to move to a smaller house at 10 Admiral Grove, Dingle. Dingle was a rough area, even by Liverpool standards. The house was condemned, only had an outside toilet and no garden, but they stayed for 20 years. Ringo's paternal grandparents still lived nearby on Madryn Street and they shared his upbringing with his mother. He attended the nearby St. Silas primary school but was never very happy there.

Richard was a sickly child and at six and a half his appendix burst. An ambulance was called and he was rushed to hospital. On the operating table they discovered that he had peritonitis. He fell into a coma that lasted for ten weeks. During that time his mother was repeatedly warned that he might not recover.

> **“**We were the first generation that didn't go into the army. I missed the call up by, like, 10 months, and so we were allowed, as these teenagers, not to be regimented and turn into these musicians.**”**
>
> *Ringo Starr*

▲ Ringo (with a beard, right) with Rory Storm and the Hurricanes at Butlins.

When he came round he had long periods when he was barely conscious. It made his mother very possessive. He had to stay in the sanatorium for a year before he recovered sufficiently to leave and even then he was still recovering and didn't go back to school for two years.

When Richard returned to school he had fallen well behind with his lessons. Embarrassed, he tried to bunk off whenever he could. He started to hate school and couldn't read until he was nine. At the age of 11 his stepfather-to–be, Harry Graves, came into his life.

Two years later Harry married Elsie. Initially jealous of his mother's split affection, Richard came to really like Harry, who encouraged him to listen to and enjoy a wide range of music.

Academically behind, he was sent to Dingle Vale Secondary Modern School at the age of 12. A 30-minute walk away from home, he rarely attended anyway. There were other temptations along the way, not least of which was a music store full of instruments.

▲ Rory Storm and the Hurricanes at the Jive Hive (aka St. Luke's Church Hall) in August 1961. (L–R) Rory Storm (born Alan Caldwell), Johnny Guitar (born Johnny Byrne), Ringo Starr (born Richard Starkey), Lu Walters (born Wally Eymond).

> 66 I'm not the creative one. I know that. If Rory Storm hadn't come along … and then The Beatles … I would have continued running around in teddyboy gangs. … I'm glad I'm not, of course. It'll be nice to be part of history. 99
>
> *Ringo Starr*

When he was 13, Richard's health failed him again. He contracted chronic pleurisy that developed into tuberculosis and had to stay for ten months in a sanatorium. While there, as part of the therapy, a teacher came in with a selection of instruments, but Richard would only play if he was given the drums. He even joined the hospital band. When he came out of hospital, as a treat his grandparents took him to the Isle of Man. While there, they went to the cinema to see *Rock Around the Clock*. Even though he was too weak to join in, he loved it when the audience went wild.

He bought his first drum for 30 shillings: "a huge, one-sided bass drum," which he loved playing at parties (using two sticks of firewood) alongside his grandfather, uncles, and their friends, until they got fed up with his noise and threw him out.

By this time Richard had decided to become a sailor and travel around the world; they were the best-dressed and most exotic men in Liverpool and all the lads looked up to them. His first job was as a messenger boy working on the railways, but that only lasted for about five weeks because he failed the medical and had to leave. For a while he worked on the *St. Tudno*, a pleasure steamer that worked between Liverpool and North Wales, before he went to work as an apprentice engineer at H. Hunt & Son, principally to avoid being conscripted into the armed services.

He loved rock'n'roll music and became a real Teddy boy (unlike John who only posed as one) around the age of 16. In Dingle you had to belong to a gang or be a target for everyone. In spite of gang membership, he was still beaten up a number of times. He didn't like the physicality and boredom of gang culture and thanks to his love of music was able to leave all that behind by the time he turned 19.

As a young teenager Richard loved skiffle, the contemporary fad. For Christmas his family clubbed together to buy him a second-hand £12 drum kit. It had a snare, bass drum, hi-hat, a small tom-tom, a bass-drum pedal, and a top cymbal. He set it up in his bedroom, but after complaints from the neighbors looked for a band to join. In 1957, he started a band—the Eddie Clayton Skiffle Group—with Roy Trafford and Eddie Miles, his friends and workmates from H. Hunt & Son. They started playing clubs, parties, and weddings, almost always for nothing, just to get the practice. Roy and Eddie were happy to play as a hobby, but Richard wanted to become professional. He moved on to play with other Liverpool groups and became semi-professional, working as an engineer during the day and drumming at night.

He finally auditioned for Rory and the Hurricanes and got the job even though they had reservations about him. According to Ringo himself, "When I went for the audition I looked a bit rough: I was still in my black drape jacket with my hair back, looking like a Ted, so they were a bit insecure about me." He toured with them around Britain and abroad. He wasn't earning much, but it was enough to buy his own car at 18: a red and white Standard Vanguard. Suddenly, transporting his drum kit to and from gigs became much easier.

In 1959 Richard turned professional, earning £16 a week (instead of the £6 as an engineer) playing with Rory Storm and the Hurricanes at the Rock and Calypso Ballroom at Butlins holiday camp. He played there for three months over the summer and this is

when he took the stage name Ringo Starr. He earned enough to be able to buy a better car, a Zephyr Zodiac. After the season finished he picked up odd jobs here and there but was often unemployed.

In 1962 Rory Storm and the Hurricanes toured U.S. Army bases in France. They were popular and were offered a residency in Hamburg. While playing there, Ringo met John, Paul, and George. Occasionally he was asked to play with The Beatles when their drummer, Pete Best, was unavailable. When Best was sacked by Brian Epstein, Ringo was given the job. Paul said later that he always thought of Ringo as the grown-up in the group because he was two years older than John and already had a car as well as a suit and a beard!

▼ Ringo quickly fitted in and became a close friend.

The Inner Circle

Usually when a band starts up there are a number of non-musical friends who take on other necessary roles such as roadies, publicists, and bookers. In this The Beatles were no different. Many of their inner circle were friends from their early days in Liverpool and some of them stayed around throughout their career. Many of them have written reminiscences of their time with The Beatles.

◀ The Beatles rehearse for a performance on *The Ed Sullivan Show*. Neil Aspinall stands in for bed-ridden George Harrison, February 9, 1964.

▼ Mal Evans, road manager from 1963.

Mal Evans
May 27, 1935–January 5, 1976

Mal was born in Liverpool and became a professional telephone engineer. During his lunch breaks he often went to the Cavern Club where he heard the band and became a Beatles fan. He got to know George, who then recommended him to the Cavern's manager as a prospective bouncer—he was burly and 6ft. 6in. tall.

Mal was a constant presence throughout the band's life. He drove them around, fetched and carried for them, went out and bought food and clothes as requested, as well as regularly putting his considerable bulk between them and their fans. But more than this he was also their friend. He and Neil Aspinall would even sign autographs for the band when they were busy!

In July 1966 while touring the Philippines, The Beatles (actually Brian Epstein) refused a breakfast invitation to meet the dictator's wife Imelda Marcos. Their police protection evaporated and The Beatles had to make their way to Manila airport with only their entourage. There they were met by a hostile crowd. Mal got beaten and kicked as he tried to protect the band and was then, with the press officer, ordered off the plane and only allowed back on after Brian Epstein had handed over all the money they had earned.

Neil Aspinall
October 13, 1941–March 24, 2008

The other principal insider was Neil, who went to school with George and Paul at the Liverpool Institute and was their first road manager and gofer. When he left school with good grades he studied accountancy and then got a job as a trainee accountant. He left to become The Beatles' permanent road manager and drive them around in April 1962 when they got their third Hamburg residency. The pay was better.

When Mal Evan joined the entourage in 1963, Neil was promoted to personal assistant and did more important tasks than just driving, although he still did that. He became particular friends with Pete Best (he had an affair and a baby with Pete's mother Mona) and almost left the Beatles when the latter was sacked. However, he was soon working closely with Brian Epstein passing on his thoughts and comments to the group. He was the one, with assistance from Mal, who found the photographs for the montage on the cover of *Sgt. Pepper*.

In August 1968 when Brian Epstein died, Neil was asked to take on the management of Apple Corps. It had only been going for five months and he agreed to be the interim manager until a better candidate came along. It was a big job as there was no clear paperwork for any of The Beatles' business commitments. When Allan Klein became manager he sacked Neil, but the Beatles quickly got him reinstated. One of Neil's biggest contributions was to have the foresight to trademark the Apple name worldwide.

Neil stayed deeply involved in Apple business until his death in 2008 from lung cancer. He advised the

▲ Press agent Derek Taylor leans in to advise John during a press conference as George answers a question in 1964.

After The Beatles stopped touring, Mal continued to work for them in the studio, running their various errands and working as a semi-bodyguard. On occasion he added his voice to recordings and even some instrumentation and odd sounds as required. He even appeared briefly in three of their films. In 1973 he separated from his wife and moved to Los Angeles (near John). One unhappy day he was playing with an air rifle, it was reported to the police who mistook it for a rifle and shot him dead.

individual Beatles professionally and supervised the music videos and merchandising of Beatles product. He also advised and helped to sort out both John and George's estates.

▲ Paul on a train between Munich and Hamburg in 1966. Tony Barrow is in the background.

Other insiders

In the 1960s Brian Epstein's personal assistant was **Peter Brown**, whom he knew through the family business in Liverpool. Brian made him a director of NEMS Enterprises and he was a close confidant of both Epstein and the individual Beatles. In 1968 when Brian set up Apple Corps, Peter was integral to the development and as a consequence became a board member. Then when Brian died, Peter took over many of his day-to-day duties and kept things running as smoothly as possible.

As a close personal friend of the Beatles, Peter was a witness at Paul and Linda's wedding and best man for John and Yoko. When The Beatles split and went their own ways, Peter became President and Chief Executive of the theatrical Robert Stigwood Organisation.

Tony Bramwell grew up in Liverpool where he was a close friend of George. Soon he got to know Paul and in due course John. Then one day he bumped into George on the bus: the band had just come back from Hamburg and were off to another gig. He offered to carry George's guitar so he could get in for free. John and Paul asked him to carry theirs as well, and from then on he became their tour manager. When Brian Epstein became their manager he offered Tony a full time job at NEMS where he became his right-hand man. Epstein bought the Saville Theatre in Piccadilly, London and put Tony in charge of booking: he booked Jimi Hendrix's first UK gig.

In 1968 he was made head of Apple Films where he made promotional films for The Beatles and the other Apple acts. After The Beatles broke up he became CEO of Apple Records and then a successful independent record promoter.

▲ Ray McFall (owner of the Cavern) and Bob Wooler (a DJ at the club who introduced the band to Brian Epstein). outside the Club. John and Wooler had a punch up at Paul's 21st.

Another member of the inner circle was another Liverpudlian, **Derek Taylor**. Working as a journalist for the *Liverpool Daily Post* and *Echo*, he was sent to cover a Beatles concert where he was expecting to belittle the phenomenon. Instead, he was thrilled by their exciting act and wrote a piece extolling their charisma. Soon afterwards The Beatles asked to meet him and they became close and trusted friends.

Derek's newspaper decided to run a Beatles column supposedly authored by George Harrison but ghostwritten by Derek. The job turned into a collaboration and close friendship, with George providing the stories and Derek professionally writing them up. Then in 1964 Brian Epstein hired Derek as The Beatles press officer and media liaison. He also helped Brian write his autobiography, *A Cellarful of Noise*, by transcribing and writing up Brian's taped

reminiscences. He resigned from his job after the 1964 tour of America and moved to California where he started his own PR company promoting the likes of the Beach Boys and The Byrds.

Derek returned to England in 1968 as press officer for Apple Corps and an important member of the company until he left. In 1980 he helped George write his autobiography and then he wrote his own three years later. Derek rejoined Apple in the 1990s to market their various projects. He was still working for Apple when he died of cancer in September 1997.

Alistair Taylor wasn't quite a Liverpudlian as he came from nearby Runcorn. After working at Liverpool docks he was taken on by Brian Epstein at NEMS as his personal assistant for £10 a week. The legend goes that he bluffed Brian Epstein into ordering The Beatles disk "My Bonnie" and so brought them to his attention. On November 9, 1961, Alistair and Brian walked round the corner from NEMS to the Cavern Club to see The Beatles. Alistair thought they were sensational, even in their rough black leather jackets and swathed in cigarette smoke. Brian agreed and within a few weeks had become their manager.

The Beatles soon gave Alistair the nickname "Mr. Fixit," because that was what he was good at, sorting out all manner of diverse problems. He was meticulous in attention to detail and absolutely reliable. He was at their side for many of their most momentous times. Three months after Brian died, John asked Alistair to become General Manager for Apple. But when Allen Klein joined Apple, Alistair was one of the 16 people sacked in the first purge. He was not told why. He then went to work for Elton John, promoting his first two albums. After moving to Derbyshire with his wife in 1973 he did a variety of jobs. He died after a short illness in 2004.

▲Alexis Mardas (aka Magic Alex) was in the inner circle for a while from 1966 after he met John. Here he and George are seen at Hearthrow, January 16, 1968, having returned from Bombay where George had been recording the soundtrack to the film *Wonderwall*.

◀ ▲(R–L) Ringo Starr, Geoff Emerick (who has just won a Grammy for his work on *Sgt. Pepper*), and George Martin. Emerick took over from "Hurricane" Smith after *Rubber Soul* and worked with band until 1968. Later, he won a grammy for his work on Paul's *Band on the Run*.

◀Terry Doran worked with Brian, and as a Beatles aide. He ran Brydor Cars and was the man from the motor trade mentioned in the Beatles song "She's Leaving Home."

Brian Epstein
September 19, 1934–August 27, 1967

Brian Epstein was an impresario and businessman long before he met The Beatles, managing Liverpudlian acts such as Gerry and The Pacemakers, Cilla Black, and Billy J. Kramer: but it was with The Beatles that he made his name.

Born Brian Samuel Epstein into a Russian-Jewish Liverpool family on September 19, 1934, he was not obviously musical. After leaving school he joined the family furniture shop I. Epstein and Sons (later

> 66 Well, I don't know about the dizzy heights, but I always thought they were going to be pretty big. 99
>
> *Brian Epstein*

expanded to become NEMS, North End Music Stores). In late December 1952 Brian was conscripted into two years' National service. He served in the Royal Army Service Corps and was posted to London. He was discharged after ten months for being "emotionally and mentally unfit." He returned to the family fold where his parents learnt about his homosexuality and reluctantly allowed him to return to London to study acting at RADA (Royal Academy of Dramatic Art). There he was a contemporary of Albert Finney and Peter O'Toole but he discovered that he was too much of a businessman to enjoy acting. He dropped out and returned to Liverpool before the first year was complete.

His father put him in charge of the ground floor of the latest NEMS shop on Great Charlotte Street, Liverpool, which he turned into one of the biggest music stores in the north of England. He was then given a second shop to run at 12–14 Whitechapel. It was just down the street and round the corner from the Cavern Club. In the nearby rival department store worked Peter Brown (later a confidant of The Beatles) who Brian soon poached to join NEMS. At around the same time Brian was given a regular music

▲ Brian Epstein was instrumental in the band's success.

▲ Brian Epstein's "boys": (L–R) The Beatles, Gerry and The Pacemakers (Gerry Marsden, Freddy Marsden, Les Chadwick, Les McGuire), Billy J. Kramer and The Dakotas (Robin McDonald, Mike Maxfield, Billy J. Kramer, Ray Jones, Tony Mansfield) with Brian (center at top; on right center and below), June 20, 1963.

column called "Record Releases by Brian Epstein of NEMS" in the new *Mersey Beat* magazine and started contributing from the third issue.

Being on such close terms with the Liverpool music scene, Brian soon noticed the name of The

Beatles around the city. The band was even on the front cover of the second issue of *Mersey Beat*. As an occasional visitor to the Cavern Club—even though he was not a fan of pop music, this was business— Brian kept an eye on the performers there and on one occasion made a special effort to catch The Beatles for himself. He later claimed that "I was immediately struck by their music, their beat, and their sense of humor on stage." On meeting them after the gig in their tiny dressing room, he also warmed to them personally.

> ## "After Brian Epstein died we collapsed." *John Lennon*

Over the next few days he started thinking about managing them. He went to every one of their gigs over the next three weeks and contacted their previous manager, Allan Williams, to check that he was no longer contracted to them. Williams warned Epstein to stay well away from The Beatles as they had not honored some payment that he felt entitled to from their Hamburg gigs.

After three meetings in December 1961, The Beatles came to an arrangement with Brian to manage them and signed a five-year contract on December 10, 1961, at Pete Best's house. Brian didn't sign it, he said later, so they could tear it up if they wanted to. On January 1, 1962, they went down to London to audition for Decca Records and make a demo which Brian paid for.

As Paul, George, and Pete were all under 21 they needed their guardians' consent to sign a management contract. Agreements were made (Aunt Mimi's veto didn't matter as John was over 21) and on January 24, 1962, Brian Epstein legally became manager of The Beatles as NEMS Enterprises, taking 25 percent of their gross income as his cut. The remainder was to be shared equally among The Beatles after all expenses had been taken out.

One by one Brian visited all the record companies in London. They all agreed to see him because he represented an important northern record outlet, but one by one they rejected The Beatles. He contacted EMI and they turned him down. Eventually he was directed to George Martin, head of EMI's Parlophone label (he had been on holiday before when Brian visited EMI), who agreed to listen to his tapes of The Beatles although he couldn't meet them personally

as they were playing a residency in Hamburg. When George Martin said yes, Brian sent a telegram to Hamburg with the good news. However, shortly afterward Brian was given the dirty job of sacking Pete Best by the other Beatles, not something he wanted to do.

Brian started to influence their stage appearance: he made them more professional—they started using set lists, they had to stop swearing on stage … and drinking and smoking and even eating as they had been known to do. Eventually he got them out of their leather jackets and denim jeans and into suits. He got them to bow at the end of each song and eventually even got them into matching suits which gave them their image of being nice, clean-cut boys. They also started to play in better venues and even to get slightly more money. Their profile was starting to improve.

In 1964 Brian moved NEMS Enterprises (created in 1962 especially to manage The Beatles and other acts) to London where it employed a staff of 25. Brian booked all the shows, concerts, and TV appearances; furthermore, he used his own NEMS acts as openers for The Beatles. He was making money as the booking agent, the promoter, and the manager for all the acts on the bill.

As The Beatles' fame grew, Brian was increasingly busy with scheduling their various enterprises. He was not pleased when they announced that they would no longer tour after their last live concert at Candlestick Park in San Francisco on August 29, 1966.

The Beatles all trusted Brian implicitly (perhaps too much so, admitted John) and never even bothered to read the contracts he asked them to sign. One time when the Beatles were earning £25 each a week, Brian proposed that he would contract to give each of them a guaranteed fixed wage of £50 a week for life; they flatly refused as they knew they were worth far more.

When John married Cynthia on August 23, 1962, he was their best man and paid for the wedding lunch. He became godfather to their son Julian. His homosexuality was an open secret and not a problem for any of the Beatles, in fact they seem to have been very protective of him.

In October 1964 Brian published his autobiography, *A Cellarful of Noise,* ghost-written by his assistant Derek Taylor. In it he describes the early years of The Beatles.

Throughout his time with The Beatles Brian took stimulants, at first just to give himself energy and to keep himself awake. But his drug use increased and he made frequent visits to the Priory rehabilitation clinic in west London. A few weeks before he died he was there for chronic insomnia and dependency on amphetamines and then had to attend his father's funeral in Liverpool. On August 27, 1967, Brian Epstein died from an overdose of barbiturates at his home in Chapel Street. The inquest ruled his death accidental and probably caused by a build up of sleeping pills and alcohol.

When they heard the awful news the Beatles were in Bangor, Wales, with guru Maharishi Mahesh Yogi. They were all devastated: Jimi Hendrix cancelled a concert that he was due to give at Brian's Saville Theatre out of respect. The Beatles stayed away from his funeral not wanting to turn it into a media circus. He was buried in the Long Lane Jewish cemetery, Aintree, Liverpool. On October 17 all the Beatles attended a memorial service for him at the New

▲ John and Cynthia leave the New London Synagogue after the memorial service for Brian Epstein October 17, 1967.

London Synagogue in St John's Wood, London.

When Brian died his brother Clive took over NEMS as the second biggest shareholder. Without Brian the Beatles had no one to solve their differences and sort out their problems. They quickly started to quarrel and drift apart and their business dealings rapidly got out of hand.

> 66 George Martin had a very great musical knowledge and background and he could translate for us and suggest a lot of things. 99
>
> *John Lennon*

◄ George Martin at Abbey Road Studios, October 1964.

George Henry Martin
January 3, 1926–

George Martin has often been dubbed the "Fifth Beatle" for his ubiquity as their producer throughout their career and for his unique and invaluable contributions to their distinctive music.

He was born in the Highbury neighborhood of Islington, North London. George's interest in music was sparked very early, but he did not consider a career in music until he had studied the piano and oboe at the Guildhall School of Music and Drama. He joined the BBC's classical music department, then EMI in 1950 as a music assistant, for Parlophone Records.

At that time the headline label at EMI was Columbia Records led by Norrie Paramor, who had the likes of Cliff Richard and Helen Shapiro on his books and

huge success at the top of the charts with his string-driven productions. In complete contrast, Parlophone was a rather obscure label specializing in British folk, musical cast recordings, baroque, and general classical music. In 1955 at the age of 29 George was put in charge of it, making him the youngest manager of any EMI label. This backwater area of the company away from the close scrutiny of the money men gave him an unprecedented amount of freedom.

George Martin also produced jazz music and novelty records including various comedy outings. However he wanted to broaden Parlophone's range by securing a popular singer or band. He had already had some small success without finding anyone special. One day in 1962 he was contacted about Brian Epstein and told that he managed a promising new band called The Beatles. The group had already been turned down by most of the leading labels but they sounded intriguing. Martin agreed to see Epstein on February 13, 1962: he wasn't impressed by their tape but he did like the sound of the John and Paul's harmonies and asked to see Epstein again, but this time at his EMI studios in Abbey Road.

After listening again and convinced by Epstein's belief in the band, George gave them a recording contract without having met them or even seen them play—they were in Hamburg at the time. But crucially he hadn't signed it; he wanted to meet them and hear them play first, so he gave them an hour in the studio. On June 6, 1962, The Beatles auditioned in studio 3 in Abbey Road for George Martin. Four songs were recorded without Martin being present; he then listened to the tape afterward. Both he and the engineers were dubious about Pete Best's drumming and the quality of their self-penned songs. Now in his early thirties, George was a good fifteen years older than The Beatles and much more staid, nevertheless they warmed to each other. On talking to them he liked their wit, rapport, and general good humor, and decided to take a chance and sign them.

On May 9, 1962, Brian Epstein sent The Beatles a telegram saying that they had been signed to Parlophone. The deal was not great: Parlophone gave The Beatles one penny for every record sold which was then split four ways between them, while singles sold outside the UK got them half a penny—again split four ways. George Martin was not risking much with his contract. It was not until January 27, 1966, that Brian Epstein was able to renegotiate The Beatles royalty rate with Parlophone when they signed a new nine-year contract. This included a 25 percent royalty to be paid to NEMS for the duration of the contract—due even if The Beatles did not renew the pending management contract with Brian Epstein.

On September 4 George Martin got them into the studio again but this time to record a hit single. Much to John and Paul's disgust, Martin wanted them to record "How Do You Do It" rather than one of their own songs. They did so, but they convinced him that they should release their own material—"Love Me Do" being the song chosen. Brian Epstein was so taken with George Martin that he brought his other acts to him to produce—notably Cilla Black, Billy J. Kramer and Gerry and The Pacemakers. Within weeks the Liverpool sound was dominating the charts.

The Beatles and Epstein trusted George Martin's judgement and he responded by providing the expertise and knowledge that they lacked. He scored keyboard fills, instrumental interludes, and orchestral pieces as required in collaboration with the band so that professional session musicians could play the music required. When needed he also played piano on some tracks. He also wrote the entire orchestral score for the films *Hard Day's Night* and *Yellow Submarine*. George Martin was always willing to experiment with new sounds and techniques, and contributed integrally to the sounds that The Beatles conjured.

By the mid-1960s George Martin was making more money for EMI than any other label, but he was annoyed at they way the company treated him so he left, along with two other producers. Together with another former EMI producer they formed Associated Independent Recording (AIR). So when The Beatles insisted on working with Martin EMI had to hire him back as an independent producer.

When The Beatles fell out so catastrophically with each other during the making of *Let It Be*, George became part of the collateral damage. The recordings were shelved and then Phil Spector controversially remastered them for the album release. George was surprised when Paul phoned to ask him to produce *Abbey Road*: he agreed providing that they took direction from him and did not fall out among themselves. They promised and the sessions went surprisingly well.

64

> ❝… as close as we can get to their early live set. ❞

Neil McCormick

The first Beatles album was recorded in four, three-hour or so long sessions across three days in September and November 1962 and in February 1963 for Parlophone at the EMI Studios in Abbey Road, London. The engineer was Norman "Hurricane" Smith. (He was until after *Rubber Soul*.) For their efforts each band member was paid the Musician's Union standard fee of £7.10s (£7.50): the entire recording cost George Martin around £800.

Please Please Me was released in the UK on March 22, 1963: in the US most of the songs were initially released on *Introducing The Beatles* in 1964.

Fourteen songs were needed for the album—in the UK it was usual for 12-inch LPs to have seven a side—

and eight of the fourteen were written by Lennon/McCartney. In order to fill the album time they virtually recorded their entire live set from the Cavern Club.

The cover photograph was taken by Angus McBean looking down the stairwell inside EMI's headquarters in Manchester Square, London, and shows four eager-looking, fresh-faced young men. The album was rush-released on March 22, 1963, to follow up on the chart successes of the single hit "Please Please Me" and the less successful (No.17) single "Love Me Do."

PLEASE PLEASE ME

Side 1
1 "I Saw Her Standing There"
2 "Misery"
3 "Anna (Go to Him)" (Arthur Alexander)
4 "Chains" (Gerry Goffin, Carole King)
5 "Boys" (Luther Dixon, Wes Farrell)
6 "Ask Me Why"
7 "Please Please Me"

Side 2
1 "Love Me Do"
2 "P.S. I Love You"
3 "Baby It's You" (Mack David, Barney Williams, Burt Bacharach)
4 "Do You Want To Know A Secret"
5 "A Taste Of Honey" (Bobby Scott, Ric Marlow)
6 "There's A Place"
7 "Twist And Shout" (Phil Medley, Bert Russell)

▲ April 8, 1963: George Martin and The Beatles with their first silver disc, for sales of more than 250,000 copies of the single *Please Please Me*.

◀ "Twist and Shout" was recorded for *Please Please Me*, and was also produced as an EP—this was the EP's cover photograph.

> " … they sound not like a relic from a forgotten era of the 60s, but as thrilling and daring as they must have once done blaring from a Dansette in a suburban bedroom. You'd have to have cloth ears not to understand what the fuss was about. "

Alexis Petridis (The Guardian)

The Beatles recorded their second studio album between July and October 1963 at the EMI Studios in London with the same team of George Martin as producer and "Hurricane" Smith as the engineer. With their growing popularity the album had advance orders for half a million copies by the time Parlophone released it in late November; in the US it was released in January 1964 as *Meet The Beatles* (with fewer and some different tracks).

With The Beatles stayed at No.1 in the album charts for 21 weeks and became only the second album to make a million sales in the UK (*South Pacific* was the first). The album contained six cover songs, seven Lennon/McCartney and one Harrison song ("Don't Bother Me").

The cover photograph was taken by ex-photo journalist Robert Freeman, The Beatles favorite photographer at the time. This was also the first time that The Beatles themselves had any input into the album cover itself. They wanted something reminiscent of the pictures taken of them in Hamburg—and the stark, black portraits were the result, with the four of them wearing black turtleneck jumpers and photographed against a black background. The artwork proved very influential and the simple styling was much copied by other designers and photographers.

WITH THE BEATLES

Side 1
1 "It Won't Be Long"
2 "All I've Got To Do"
3 "All My Loving"
4 "Don't Bother Me"
5 "Little Child"
6 "Till There was You" (Meredith Wilson)
7 "Please Mister Postman" (Georgia Dobbins, William Garrett, Freddie Gorman, Brian Holland, Robert Bateman)

Side 2
1 "Roll Over Beethoven" (Chuck Berry)
2 "Hold Me Tight"
3 "You Really Got A Hold On Me" (Smokey Robinson)
4 "I Wanna Be Your Man"
5 "Devil In Her Heart" (Richard Drapkin)
6 "Not A Second Time"
7 "Money (That's what I Want)" (Janie Bradford, Berry Gordy)

▶ In the US, *With The Beatles* was released by EMI subsidiary Capitol as *Meet The Beatles* on January 20, 1964. It and the single "I Want to Hold Your Hand" went gold. Here Alan Livingston, president of Capitol Records, and The Beatles display the gold records.

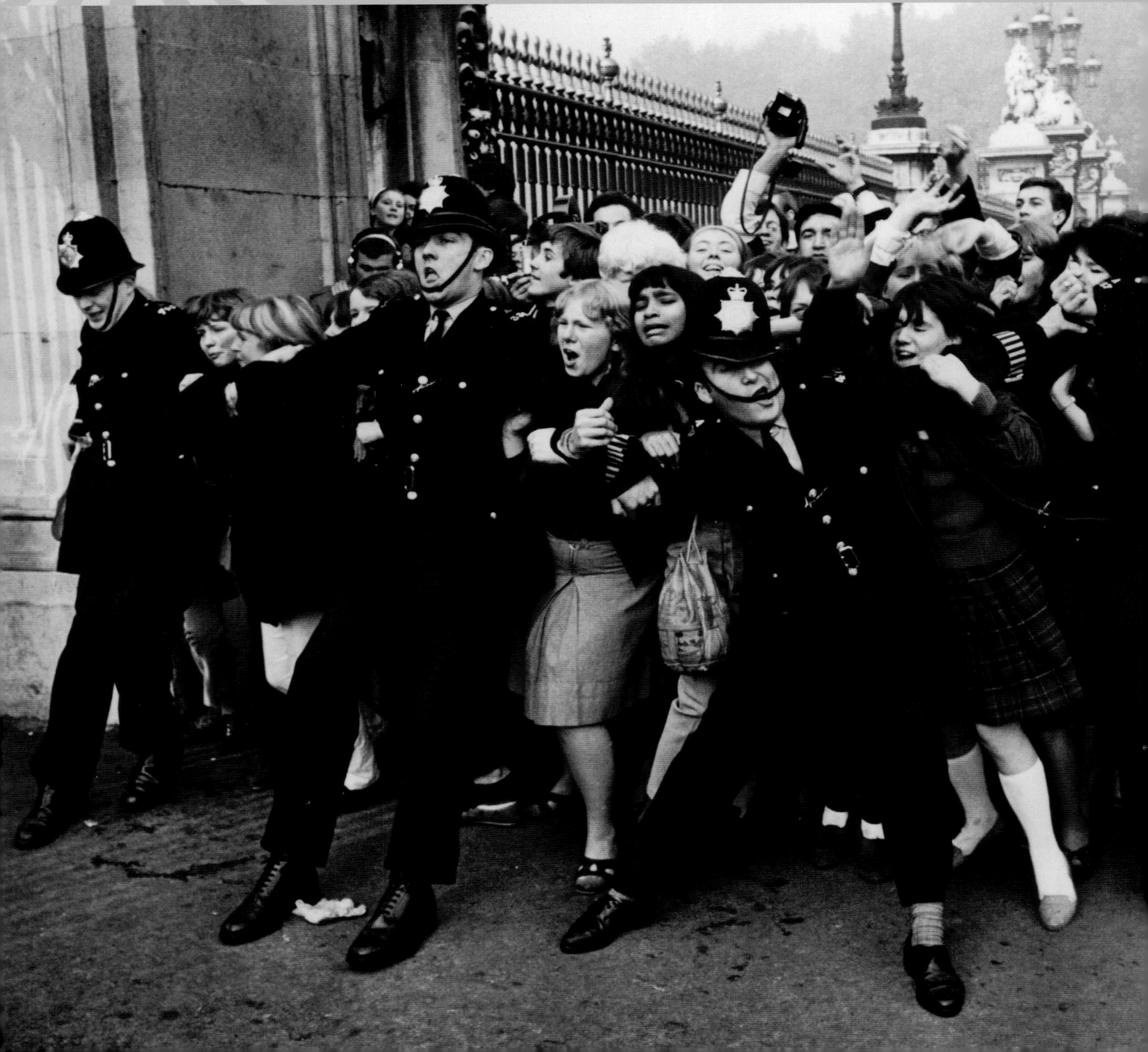

BEATLEMANIA
1964-65

> "I have never seen any scenes to compare with the bedlam that was occasioned by their debut. Broadway was jammed with people for almost eight blocks. They screamed, yelled, and stopped traffic. It was indescribable."
>
> *Ed Sullivan*

◄ Beatlemania in 1965—police keep back a crowd of young fans outside Buckingham Palace, as The Beatles receive their MBEs.

Timeline

1964

January 1—*The Jack Paar Show* plays film of the band performing "She Loves You," the first time The Beatles are seen by America.

January 3—US single re-release of "Please, Please Me" with B side "From Me To You" by Vee Jay. It reaches No.3 and sells over a million copies.

January 12—The Beatles appear for a second time on TV's *Val Parnell's Sunday Night at the London Palladium*. What a difference three months makes. This time they headline and play out the show with five songs.

January 14—the band flies to Paris. First off there's a concert at the Cinéma Cyrano in Versailles on the 15th before a three-week residency at the Olympia Theater.

January 20—Capitol release *With The Beatles* under the title *Meet The Beatles*. It goes gold on February 3 and sells 3.65 million copies in two months.

January 27—MGM releases "My Bonnie/"The Saints" as by "The Beatles and Tony Sheridan." It reaches No. 26.

February 7—another EP release: *All My Loving*, which reaches No.1 on the UK EP chart and No.12

▲January 9, 1964: Beatles' roadie and future MD of Apple Corps, Neil Aspinall (far right) with the band.

on the singles chart. On the same day, The Beatles make their way through thousands of fans and leave Heathrow airport on Pan Am flight 101. They arrive in New York to a similar crowd.

February 8—after a press conference in New York's Central Park, the band (without George who is feeling unwell) rehearses for *The Ed Sullivan Show*.

February 9—another rehearsal for the show to be broadcast

live that evening. The band also records a segment for another show to be broadcast on February 23. The Beatles' first major US TV performance attracts 73 million viewers.

February 11—The Beatles take the train to Washington, DC, play at the Washington Coliseum, and attend a cocktail party at the British Embassy.

February 12—Back in New York City they are greeted by a crowd of 10,000 before they play two shows at Carnegie Hall.

February 13—The Beatles fly to Miami, rehearse for *The Ed Sullivan*

Show on the 14th and 15th, the day *Meet The Beatles* begins an eleven-week run at the top of the U.S. album chart.

February 16—*The Ed Sullivan Show* is broadcast live to 70 million Americans.

February 18—a publicity coup: The Beatles meet Cassius Clay training in Miami for the fight against Sonny Liston that saw him win the WBC Heavyweight Championship.

February 20—in the US "Twist And Shout"/"There's A Place" is released by Tollie Records (a subsidiary of Vee Jay). It sells over a million copies and reaches No.2.

February 21—"She Loves You" reaches No.1 on the US charts the day the band flies home.

February 23—third (taped) Ed Sullivan program airs: after Ed's intro they play "Twist and Shout" and "Please Please Me" and close with "I Want to Hold Your Hand."

February 25—the band finishes recording "Can't Buy Me Love" at Abbey Road (on George's 21st birthday).

February 28—the second *From Us To You* radio show is recorded at the BBC's Piccadilly Studios in London. It will be broadcast with Alan Freeman as host on March 30.

March 2–April 24—The Beatles film *A Hard Day's Night*, although it was untitled when they started. They have to join Equity, the actors' union, first. They meet Pattie Boyd, one of the schoolgirls in the train sequences.

▼The Beatles in concert at the Olympia in Paris, January 16, 1964.

71

▲ The Beatles return from Paris.

March 16—Capitol releases "Can't Buy Me Love"/"You Can't Do That." Advance orders are 1.7 million and it's certified gold on March 31.
March 19—the band records "Can't Buy Me Love" for the BBC's T*op of the Pops* (it airs on March 25) and then attend the 12th annual Variety Club of GB awards at the Dorchester where they receive the

Show Business Personalities of 1963 award.
March 20—"Can't Buy Me Love"/"You Can't Do That" released in UK. It will reach No.1 and sell 1.5 million copies.
Ready, Steady, Go! gains its highest ratings and features live interviews with The Beatles and three songs: "Can't Buy Me Love," "You Can't Do That," and "It Won't Be Long."
March 23—John's first book, *In His Own Write*, is published.
Vee Jay releases *The Beatles*, an EP of material from the first album.
April 4—"Can't Buy Me Love" spends the first of its three weeks at No.1. *Billboard* magazine reports The Beatles now hold the top five positions on the American singles chart, with "Can't Buy Me Love" top; 2 "Twist and Shout"; 3 "She Loves You"; 4 "I Want to Hold Your Hand"; 5 "Please, Please Me."
April 10—Capitol releases *The Beatles Second Album* which goes gold on April 13 and spends five weeks at No.1.
April 18—The Beatles feature on ATV's *Morecambe and Wise Show* (recorded on December 2, 1963).
April 22—John Lennon is guest of honor at a Foyle's Literary Luncheon at the Dorchester.
April 27—another Tollie release in the US: "Love Me Do"/"P.S. I

Love You" is another million-selling No.1.
May 1—another *From Us To You* program is recorded for broadcast on Whit Monday, May 18.
May 2—John and Cynthia and George and Pattie Boyd fly to Honolulu and then Tahiti on holiday. The following day Paul and Jane Asher and Ringo and Maureen fly to the Virgin Islands. John and George return on the 26th; Paul and Ringo on the 27th.
May 11—Capitol releases an EP, *Four by The Beatles*: it has four songs from the second album and is unsuccessful.
May 18—Paul appears on *A Degree of Frost*, the first of many interviews with David Frost.

> "The concert footage as the Beatles sing 'She Loves You' … is one of the most sustained orgasmic sequences in the movies."
>
> *Roger Ebert*

Poster outside Carnegie Hall February 5, 1964.

Their arrival at New York's JFK Airport on February 7 was greeted by thousands of fans and started with a press conference.

Australia the next day.

June 12—Ringo leaves London for Australia via San Francisco while the band plays concerts in Adelaide (12/13).

June 14—Jimmy Nicol, his moment of fame over, flies home with a cheque, and a wristwatch inscribed with the words: "From The Beatles and Brian Epstein to Jimmy—with appreciation and gratitude."

June 15–18—The Beatles play three gigs in Melbourne, with Ringo back on the drums again.

June 1—the band records songs for *A Hard Day's Night* album at Abbey Road.

June 3—Ringo collapses with tonsillitis and pharyngitis and is ordered to rest. George Martin calls Jimmy Nicol to stand in. He had played the drums on an album of Beatles covers called *Beatlemania* so fitted in quickly.

June 4—The Beatles, with Jimmy Nicol, fly to Denmark to begin a world tour.

June 5—Press conference at Schipol followed by a performance for VARA-TV and two shows in Blokker in the Netherlands on the 6th.

June 7—The Beatles with Jimmy fly to Hong Kong and play a concert on June 9, flying to

June 18–20—The Beatles play three concerts at Sydney.

June 19—the release of *Long Tall Sally* as an EP leads to another No.1; it spends seven weeks at the top.

June 21—The Beatles arrive in New Zealand to play six shows—at Wellington (22/23), Auckland (24/25), Dunedin (26), and Christchurch (27)

June 26—*A Hard Day's Night* released in the US. Shorter than the UK version, as all of the US albums are until the band takes control of its own work, it sells two million and spends fourteen weeks at No.1.

June 29/30—two concerts in Brisbane end the Down Under section of their world tour; the band travels back to England on the July 1.

July 2—The Beatles arrive home and later in the day John watches on as Paul plays piano for Cilla Black recording "It's For You" at Abbey Road. George Martin produces.

July 6—premiere of *A Hard Day's Night* in London. A huge success, it is nominated for two Academy Awards.

July 7—recording session for *Top of the Pops*: two songs air on the 8th; a third on the 29th.

July 10—northern premiere of *A Hard Day's Night* in Liverpool: 200,000 line the route from Speke airport to Liverpool Town Hall where they are presented with the keys to the city. On the same day "A Hard Day's Night"/"Things We Said Today" is released as a single and *A Hard Day's Night* as an album. Selling 1.5 million copies in nine days, it becomes the fastest-selling album in history. Both single and album reach No.1 on both sides of the Atlantic.

July 13—Capitol releases "A

▲ *The Ed Sullivan* Show February 9, 1964.

Hard Day's Night"/"I Should Have Known Better" it is certified gold on August 25.

July 15—John buys Kenwood, Wood Lane, St. George's Hill Estate, Weybridge and the family moves in later that month.

July 17—three days after recording the penultimate *Top Gear* session (broadcast July 16), the band records the final *From Us To You* program for broadcast on August 3. It includes both sides of the "A Hard Day's Night" single. George buys Kinfauns in Esher, just down the road from John in Weybridge.

July 20—Capitol releases "I'll Cry Instead"/"I'm Happy Just To Dance With You" and "And I Love Her"/"If I Fell." An album released on the

▲ John and Ringo in New York, February 9, 1964.

> "Bob Dylan had heard one of our records where we said, 'I can't hide,' and he had understood, 'I get high.' He came running and said to us, 'Right, guys, I've got some really good grass.'"

John Lennon

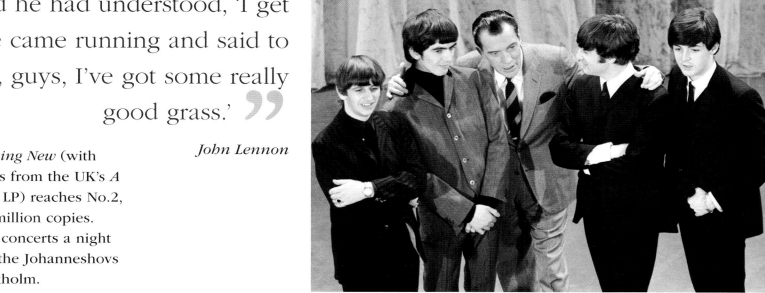

▲ On set with Ed Sullivan.

same day, *Something New* (with many of the songs from the UK's *A Hard Day's Night* LP) reaches No.2, selling over two million copies.

July 28/29—two concerts a night for two nights at the Johanneshovs Isstadion in Stockholm.

August 11—The Beatles start work on the *Beatles For Sale* album at Abbey Road, recording "Baby's in Black."

August 12—the film *A Hard Day's Night* premieres across America.

August 18–September 21—The Beatles' 25-date tour of the US and Canada starts when they fly to San Francisco via Winnipeg and Los Angeles.

August 19—The first show of the tour is a 30-minute set at the Cow Palace, which has to be stopped twice because of the number of jelly beans thrown by the 17,000+ fans. The jelly beans are a

recurring theme of The Beatles' US tours.

August 24—Capitol releases "Slow Down"/"Matchbox" as a single. It reaches No.17 on the *Billboard* singles chart.

August 28—Brian Epstein and The Beatles meet Bob Dylan in New York. The future Traveling Wilbury rolls them their first joint.

September 4—the Indonesian government bans Beatle haircuts.

September 6—30,000 watch the concert at the Olympia Stadium Detroit, the largest crowd on the US side of the tour. The

Beatles announce they won't play Florida unless the audience is desegregated.

September 7—35,000 see them in Toronto, the biggest crowd of the tour.

September 16—when they reach New Orleans the mayor declares the day Beatles Day and makes them honorary citizens.

September 17—on their day off Charles Finney gets them to play Kansas City for $150,000.

September 20—The last night of

▲ John and Cynthia on board the train for Washington DC.

the US tour is at the Paramount Theatre on Broadway in New York City. Derek Taylor and Brian Epstein argue and Taylor leaves. He will work on for three months to show his replacement, Wendy Hanson, the ropes.

September 21—The Beatles arrive at Heathrow Airport at 9.30 pm and are greeted by thousands of fans. Soon they return to Abbey Road studios to work on *Beatles For Sale*.

October 3—the band records three songs in front of a live audience for *Jack Good's Shindig!* for American TV. It broadcasts on October 7.

October 4—*A Cellarful of Noise*, Brian Epstein's autobiography, is published, ghost-written by Derek Taylor.

October 9–November 10—a month-long UK tour opens at the Gaumont Cinema in Bradford.

October 25—the band receives five Ivor Novello awards for 1963: Outstanding contribution to British music; Most broadcast song and top-selling song ("She Loves You"); Second most broadcast song ("I Want To Hold Your Hand"); Second top-selling song ("All My Loving").

November 4—in the UK Parlophone releases two EPs: one with four songs from the LP *A Hard Day's Night*. It will spend 17 weeks in the chart peaking at No.8. The other EP has four songs from the film and is more successful, spending 30 weeks in the charts, six of them at No.1.

November 23—The Beatles record a TV appearance on *Ready Steady Go!* which airs on November 27. On the other side of the Atlantic "I Feel Fine" is released by Capitol and sells a million copies in its first week. Also released, a double album: *The Beatles' Story* which combines song extracts, interviews, and a narration. It spends 17 weeks on the charts and sells a million copies inside six months.

November 16—The Beatles record "I Feel Fine" for a BBC *Top of the Pops*, which is broadcast on December 3.

November 17—the final *Top Gear* session recorded for November 26 broadcast includes both sides of the "I Feel Fine" single.

November 25—more BBC publicity for the new single when their final *Saturday Club* session is recorded. It will be broadcast on Boxing Day.

November 27—Parlophone releases "I Feel Fine"/"She's A Woman" which reaches No.1 on December 12. It spends five weeks at the top and 13 weeks in the charts.

December 1–10—Ringo spends time in University College Hospital and has his tonsils removed.

December 4—with advance orders of 750,000, Parlophone releases the *Beatles For Sale* album in the UK. The glum cover picture doesn't affect its sales and it reaches No.1 on December 19. It spends eleven weeks there in three sessions in December, February, and May. All told it spends 46 weeks in the charts.

December 9–19—George and Pattie holiday in the Bahamas.

December 15—Capitol releases its version of *Beatles for Sale* (with some track changes) as *Beatles '65*. It sells its first million inside the first week and is certified gold on December 26. To date it has sold over three million copies ...

December 24–January 16— another Beatles Christmas Show runs at the Hammersmith Odeon in London, rehearsals for which began on December 21. Compered by Jimmy Savile, most nights there are two shows and among the acts are Elkie Brooks, Gerry and the Pacemakers, and The Yardbirds—

▶ Returning home to Heathrow, February 22, 1964.

▼ Carnegie Hall, New York February 12, 1964.

◄ Labour Party leader Harold Wilson after presenting the band with their Silver Hearts at the Variety Club Awards Dorchester Hotel London, March 19, 1964.

including Eric Clapton.
December 26—"I Feel Fine" makes No.1 on the US charts. In the UK, The Beatles make their final appearance on *Saturday Club*.

1965

January 9—*Beatles '65* begins a nine-week run at No.1 on the *Billboard* chart.
January 20—Ringo proposes to Maureen while in the Ad Lib Club in Soho.
January 25–February 7—John and Cynthia join George Martin and Judy Lockhart-Smith, his future wife, on holiday in St. Moritz; George quickly breaks his foot.

George Harrison and Pattie go to Europe.
February 1—Capitol releases the last of its EPs *4 by The Beatles*. It reaches 68 in the *Billboard* chart.
February 4–February 14—Paul and Jane holiday in Hammamet, Tunisia.
February 11—Ringo marries Maureen Cox at Caxton Hall in London. Brian Epstein is best man. John and George are there but Paul is still in Tunisia.
February 15—Capitol releases "Eight Days a Week"/"I Don't Want To Spoil The Party" as a single, two tracks on *Beatles For Sale*. It sells over a million, is certified gold

in September 1965, and spends two weeks at No.1. John passes his driving test in Weybridge and afterward records "Ticket To Ride" during the first session on the new album.
February 20—the recording sessions for *Help!* are completed.
February 22—a charted BOAC Boeing 707 takes the band and costar Eleanor Bron to New Providence Island in the Bahamas to film *Eight Arms To Hold You* which will become *Help!*
February 23–March 9—filming in the Bahamas takes two weeks after which The Beatles return to London on the 10th.

◀ On the set of *Ready Steady Go!* at Television House, March 20, 1964.

"Ticket To Ride"/"Yes It Is." It will spend 12 weeks on the charts.

April 11—The Beatles top the bill at the *NME* Poll Winners concert at the Empire Pool, Wembley for the third year running. 10,000 watch them perform. It is broadcast on April 18. Straight after the concert they were driven to Teddington where they performed on the *Eamonn Andrews Show*.

April 13—at the 7th Annual Grammy Awards, The Beatles win twice: Best New Artist of 1964 and "A Hard Day's Night" wins Best Performance by a Vocal Group. The album of the same name was inducted into the Grammy Hall of Fame in 2000.

Paul buys 7 Cavendish Avenue, St. John's Wood, London for £40,000.

April 19—Capitol releases "Ticket To Ride"/"Yes It Is" and it spends eleven weeks in the charts, one of which (May 22) is at No.1.

April 24—The first of three weeks at No.1 in the UK for "Ticket To Ride," and five weeks at No.1 on the EP charts for *Beatles For Sale*.

April 28—Peter Sellers presents each of the band with a Grammy for "A Hard Day's Night" during filming at Twickenham.

March 13–March 22—no sooner are they back than they fly to Salzburg in Austria. They are greeted by a huge crowd. After a press conference they go to Obertauern where filming takes place. They return to London on the 22nd.

March 22—Capitol releases *The Early Beatles*, an album that sells over a million and is certified gold in 1975. It spends 35 weeks on the *Billboard* chart but doesn't get higher than No.43

March 24–May 11—filming for *Help!* continues off and on at Twickenham Studios and later in May on Salisbury Plain.

April 3—The Beatles appear on *Thank Your Lucky Stars*, which was recorded on March 28.

April 6—Parlophone releases the EP *Beatles For Sale*. It spends 47 weeks in the chart, six of them at No.1, in two sessions.

April 9—Parlophone releases

◀ Photocall ahead of the band's August American tour, April 26, 1964.

May 2–6—The Beatles stay in the Antrobus Arms, Amesbury while they film sequences for *Help!* on Salisbury Plain with the British Army.

May 9—the band goes to the Royal Festival Hall to watch a gig by Bob Dylan and spend time with him and Alan Ginsberg afterward at the Savoy Hotel. They get on well enough for John, Cynthia, George, and Pattie to go to Ginsberg's 39th birthday party on June 3— although they beat a hasty retreat when they find Ginsberg naked.

May 11—The last day of filming *Help!* at Cliveden House in Berkshire.

May 22—"Ticket To Ride" spends one week at the top of the *Billboard* chart.

May 26—The Beatles record their final BBC radio program, *The Beatles Invite You To Take A Ticket To Ride*, broadcast on June 7.

May 27–June 11—Paul and Jane holiday in Portugal. During the holiday he writes "Yesterday." It comes to him in a dream and will be one of the most covered songs of all time, consistently voted top or near the top pop song ever.

> "I had a piano at my bedside, and I must have dreamed it, because I tumbled out of bed and put my hands on the piano keys, and I had a tune in my head. It was just all there, a complete thing."
>
> *Paul McCartney* about "Yesterday"

▲ Performing in the one-hour TV special *Around The Beatles* on April 28.

June 3—John's Rolls-Royce Phantom V FJB111C is delivered. He and the band will use it extensively over the next few years. The famous psychedelic paint job was done by J.P. Fallon Ltd. in 1967, to the design of artist Steve Weaver. It went to America in 1970 and was donated to the Cooper-Hewitt Museum in New York City in return for a $225,000 tax credit. It ended up in Canada.

June 4— Parlophone releases the EP *Beatles For Sale 2* which spends 24 weeks on the charts peaking at No.5.

June 11—the press embargo on the Queen's Birthday Honours List

is lifted and the press report that The Beatles are to receive MBEs. Reaction is, unsurprisingly, mixed.

June 14—Capitol releases *Beatles VI*, their sixth and the ninth Beatles album so far released in the US. In spite of it being a haphazard collection of material it still sells over a million and will be certified gold on July 1. It spends 41 weeks on the charts, six at No.1

Paul starts recording "Yesterday"; it will be finalized on the 17th.

June 20–July 3—a short European tour sees three concerts in France, opening at the Palais des Sports in Paris, four in Italy, and two in Spain.

June 24—*A Spaniard in the Works*,

▲ Jimmy Nicol replaced Ringo at the start of the world tour, June 3, 1964.

▶ Convention Centre, Las Vegas, August 20, 1964.

John's second book, is published.

July 13—Paul attends the Ivor Novello awards at the Savoy and accepts five Novello awards. "Can't Buy Me Love" was awarded Most Performed Work of 1964 and the Highest Certified British Sales.

July 19—Capitol releases "Help!"/"I'm Down" and two months later it has sold a million; it spends thirteen weeks on the charts, three at No.1.

Ringo and Maureen join John in Weybridge buying Sunny Heights.

◀ After playing the Hollywood Bowl, on August 24 they had a day off in Bel Air. They visited a ranch where they were given cowboy hats, guns, and holsters.

July 23—Parlophone releases "Help!"/"I'm Down." It will sell 900,000 copies and chart for 14 weeks.

July 29—The premiere of *Help!* at the London Pavilion cinema in Piccadilly Circus. 10,000 fans turn out.

August 1—to promote the film the band appears on *Blackpool Night Out* hosted by Mike and Bernie Winters.

August 6—Parlophone releases *Help!* which will sell 2.5 million copies worldwide, entering the charts at No.1. It will stay there for 14 weeks and another 23 in the charts.

August 7—*Help!,* the UK single, starts its three-week run at No.1.

August 11—the film *Help!* opens in New York (it opened on the 9th in Chicago). It garners a pair of BAFTAs, second place in the Golden Laurels, and is nominated for a Grammy.

August 13—Capitol releases the album *Help!* on the day the band arrives in New York for its third US tour. The LP will spend 44 weeks on the charts, nine of them (from September 11) at No.1.

August 14—the band records "I Feel Fine," "I'm Down," "Act Naturally," "Ticket to Ride," "Yesterday," and "Help!" for their last live Ed Sullivan show which will air on September 12.

August 15–31—the second US tour opens with a record-breaking performance at New York's Shea Stadium in front of 55,600. Other dates include Toronto, Atlanta (August 18—a crowd of 30,000), Houston, Chicago (August 20—60,000), Minneapolis, Portland, San Diego, Los Angeles, and the last concert, on the 31st, at Cow Palace San Francisco in front of 18,000.

August 27—The Beatles meet Elvis Presley at his house in Hollywood. They get on well but a famous jam session isn't recorded and Col. Parker doesn't allow any photographs.

September 4—*Help!* spends the first of its three weeks at the top of the *Billboard* singles' chart.

September 13—Capitol releases "Yesterday"/"Act Naturally" and it storms into No.1 position on the charts, spending four weeks there from October 9. By October 20 it is certified gold.

Maureen and Ringo's son, Zak, the future drummer for Oasis and The Who, is born.

September 25—The Beatles'

Saturday morning cartoon show begins in the U.S.

October 11—in the UK, Marianne Faithfull records "Yesterday," but her version loses out on the charts to Matt Monro's.

October 12–November 15—*Rubber Soul* is recorded and mixed.

October 26—The Beatles receive their MBEs from Her Majesty The Queen at Buckingham Palace.

November 1–2—the band works on *The Music Of Lennon & McCartney*, a Granada TV special that will air nationally on

December 16.

November 23—the band records a ground-breaking set of videos for the next single (the double A side "Day Tripper"/"We Can Work It Out") and three earlier songs: "Help!," "Ticket To Ride," and "I Feel Fine." Sent to TV stations, they are used—for example—by the BBC on *Top of the Pops*.

November 25—Harrods opens

▼The Christmas Show 1964 included Sounds Incorporated, the Yardbirds, Elkie Brooks, and Freddie and the Dreamers.

Eskimo costumes for the Christmas Show … they hated them by the end of the run.

up at 22:00 just for The Beatles to Christmas shop.

December 3—Parlophone releases the single "Day Tripper"/"We Can Work It Out" and the album *Rubber Soul* on the same day that the band opens its final UK tour at Glasgow's Odeon Cinema.

December 3–12—on their last tour of the UK, The Beatles visit Glasgow (3rd), Newcastle (4th), Liverpool (5th), Manchester (7th), Sheffield (8th), Birmingham (9th), London (10th and 11th), and Cardiff (12th).

December 6—Capitol releases "Day Tripper"/"We Can Work It Out" and *Rubber Soul* (less "Drive My Car," "Nowhere Man," "What Goes On," and "If I Needed Someone").

In the UK Parlophone goes for overkill releasing an EP, *The Beatles' Million Sellers*, with "She Loves You," "I Want To Hold Your Hand," "Can't Buy Me Love," and "I Feel Fine." `even though it's old material, it still spends eleven weeks in the charts and four at No.1.

December 18—the first of five weeks at No.1 on the UK chart for million-selling "Day Tripper"/"We Can Work It Out"—which also enters the US charts.

December 25—*Rubber Soul* starts its nine-week run at the top of the UK charts. It will spend 42 weeks in the charts in total, and *Rolling Stone* magazine will place it fifth on its list of the 500 greatest albums. On the same day, it starts

a 59-week run in the US charts, selling over a million copies after nine days and, to date, over four million.

George asks Pattie to marry him.

▼The Beatles pose with their MBEs at a press conference held at the Saville Theatre London following their investiture at Buckingham Palace October 26, 1965.

◀Winners of the *Birmingham Evening Mail* competition watch the band at a recording of *Thank Your Lucky Stars*, March 28, 1965.

Wives and Girlfriends

Cynthia Lennon September 10, 1939–

John met Cynthia Powell in calligraphy class at the Liverpool College of Art. She was slightly over a year older than him, from a well-to-do family. Although he teased her about being posh, John was obviously attracted to her, and after a time they started going out although she was engaged to someone else. John was angrily possessive of her and occasionally violent. Because of their relationship, her art started to suffer and she was warned to stay away from him.

Aunt Mimi did not like her and discouraged John's interest. But she did rent out a room to her (John's old bedroom, a boxroom above the front door) at 251 Menlove Avenue after her mother moved to Canada, but Cynthia soon moved out. She failed her art-teaching diploma and soon after discovered that she was pregnant. John immediately said they should get married.

They married on August 23, 1962, at the Mount Pleasant Register Office, Liverpool: Brian Epstein was best man and Paul and George guests—neither had parents there. Cynthia was 22 and John 21. That same night The Beatles had a gig in Chester. The wedding was a closely guarded secret, Brian did not want to alienate any female fans.

John Charles Julian Lennon was born on April 8, 1963, while John was away touring and just as The Beatles really started to make it. But by 1963 the news of his marriage was out and a media frenzy followed. Cynthia only went on tour with The Beatles to America once and even got left behind in New York when the others had been whisked off. She had constant battles with jealous fans trying to harm her and make her leave John.

They left their London home for Kenwood, a large mock Tudor house in Weybridge, Surrey in July 1964. It became a meeting place for the Beatles and their many friends. Unknown to Cynthia, John was serially unfaithful. In August 1968 she sued John for divorce on hearing that Yoko was pregnant with John's child. They had had ten years together.

▲John and Cynthia, George and Pattie return from their holidays, May 25, 1964.

▶John and Cynthia in St. Moritz, January 1965.

Jane Asher
April 5, 1946–

Jane Asher was born into a prosperous London family and worked as a child actor in films from the age of six. She first met Paul McCartney in April 1963 when she reviewed a gig at the Royal Albert Hall. They soon began a five-year relationship and Paul moved into her family home at 57 Wimpole Street, London. He stayed for two years during which time Jane's mother Margaret (professor of oboe at the Guildhall School of Music and Drama) taught him to play the recorder.

They became engaged on Christmas Day 1967 and went to India together to study with the Maharishi Mahesh Yogi. All The Beatles and their wives and girlfriends liked Jane immensely. Despite being attached to a wealthy man, Jane wanted to continue her own career, but Paul wanted her to give up work altogether. Additionally, she didn't enjoy the drink and drugs scene and would stay sober while the others indulged. Their circles of friends were very different, too, nevertheless together they bought a house that needed renovation in St. John's Wood London.

However, Paul was a serial seducer and unable to stay faithful to Jane; Linda Eastman was just one of many girls he was seeing. The engagement ended after one too many infidelities: they tried a reconciliation but it didn't work. Jane Asher is the only close associate of The Beatles to have never gone on public record about their time together.

◄ Paul and Jane Asher at Luton Airport May 29, 1964.

► Paul and Jane return from Portugal early so he's in the UK when the MBE award is made public, June 11, 1965.

Mary (aka Maureen) Cox
August 4, 1946–December 30, 1994

Mo was a trainee hairdresser in Liverpool when she met Ringo at the Cavern Club and started going out with him. She was one of the fans who queued for hours outside the Cavern before opening time. She soon only had eyes for Ringo. When the other girls found out she was dating a Beatle, she was subjected to violence and once had her face raked by a jealous fan in 1963. She had to give up her job as a hairdresser because of the threats.

In June 1963 Ringo collapsed and was rushed to hospital with fever brought on by tonsillitis just before an international tour. Mo visited him every day bringing him ice cream.

They became engaged at the Ad-Lib Club in London on January 20, 1965, and within days Mo discovered she was pregnant. On February 11 they married in a quickly and quietly arranged service at the Caxton Hall Register Office, London.

◀ L–R Maureen, Cynthia, and Pattie in Obertauern, Austria, March 16, 1965.

They bought a house named Sunny Heights in St. George's Hill, Surrey, but they moved homes a number of times afterward. Mo was particularly close to Pattie Harrison and Cynthia Lennon and they often went on shopping trips and holidays together.

Zak Starkey was born on the day "Yesterday" was released, September 13, 1965. They had two more children, Jason (August 1967) and Lee (November 1970). Their marriage was over by 1970 due in part to Ringo's excessive drinking and infidelities. Mo had a brief affair with George and was discovered by Pattie. Lennon likened the encounter to being "virtual incest." Mo didn't want a divorce but it happened anyway on July 17, 1975, with Ringo cited for an affair with an American model. She tried unsuccessfully to commit suicide and Ringo later admitted to being an abusive husband.

Maureen remarried and had another daughter. She died of complications following leukemia in Seattle in December 1994. Ringo, her four children, elderly mother, and her husband were with her.

Pattie Boyd
March 17, 1944–

Patricia Anne Boyd came from Taunton in Somerset and was a successful model working in London, Paris, and New York when she met George on the film set of *A Hard Day's Night*.

Pattie was 20 when she met George but she didn't go out with him when he first asked as she had an understanding with another young man. She did say, however, that George was the most beautiful man she had ever seen. When he asked her out again and she accepted, he took her to the Garrick Club in London (Brian Epstein went with them). They quickly became an item.

George proposed to Pattie in December 1965 while they were driving through London and they married on January 21, 1966, in Esher, Surrey with Paul and Brian as best men. Meanwhile, they lived at George's house, Kinfauns also in Esher.

Pattie was interested in Indian mysticism and belonged to the Spiritual Regeneration Movement. It was through her that The Beatles met the Maharishi Mahesh Yogi in London in August 1967. The following year they all went to the Maharishi's ashram in Rishikesh, India.

▲ George and Pattie Boyd in *A Hard Day's Night* where they met.

Many men were highly attracted to Pattie, including Mick Jagger (unsuccessfully) and Eric Clapton (whom she later married for ten years). George and Pattie drifted apart through his extensive spiritual explorations, demanding work ethic, and drug use which led to his personality changes. They finally split in June 1974. However, they remained friends afterward right up to George's death. She is on record regretting letting their marriage fail, wishing they had been able to work it out. George wrote a number of songs for her including "Something" and "Isn't it a Pity."

▲Ringo with Maureen and Zak at Queen Charlotte's Maternity Hospital, London, September 14, 1965.

▶L–R Astrid Kirchherr, Maureen, and Pattie in 1965 during the filming of *A Hard Day's Night*.

▼Cynthia and Mo with The Beatles at London Airport on their way to Salzberg to film *Help!*

Fans

After The Beatles became famous they couldn't go anywhere without an escort and protection. Even from the very early days female fans could prove a handful and were especially dangerous for the women that they dated and married: Maureen Starkey once had her face badly scratched by a jealous fan and all of them were regularly kicked and shoved.

For the band the high-pitched screaming was ear-splitting. They couldn't hear themselves play and the noise was a contributing factor toward their decision

> "I've seen the stress to which they were subjected and it was absolute hell. Wherever they went, there were hordes of people trying to get hold of them, trying to get their autographs, trying to touch them."
>
> *George Martin*

The BEATLES Show TONIGHT

ALL TICKETS SOLD

NO TICKETS EXPECTED TO BE RETURNED

NO STANDING ROOM AVAILABLE

to give up touring. After some 1,400 live shows the strain had got too much. The fans in the US would throw jelly beans; gifts were as well, and could became lethal objects when thrown with a will. Paul was once hit in the face by a cigarette lighter and had to play on with a closed eye for the next couple of days. People were desperate to get at them, to get to know them, give them things, sleep with them. George said, "The only place we ever got any peace was when we got in the suite and locked ourselves in the bathroom."

Paul mused that people thought that fame imposed wisdom on them "We're constantly being asked all sorts of profound questions. But we are not very profound people. People say, "What do you think of the H-Bomb … What do I think of the H-Bomb? Well, here's an answer with the full weight of five O Levels and one A Level behind it: I don't agree with it."

Beatles' fans were great letter writers: they had to spend hours answering fan mail that came in from all over the world.

▲ George's 21st birthday: fan-club secretary Anne Collingham
helps him sort through the sacks of greeting cards and parcels,
February 25, 1964.
◀ Poster outside the Odeon Leeds, November 3, 1963.

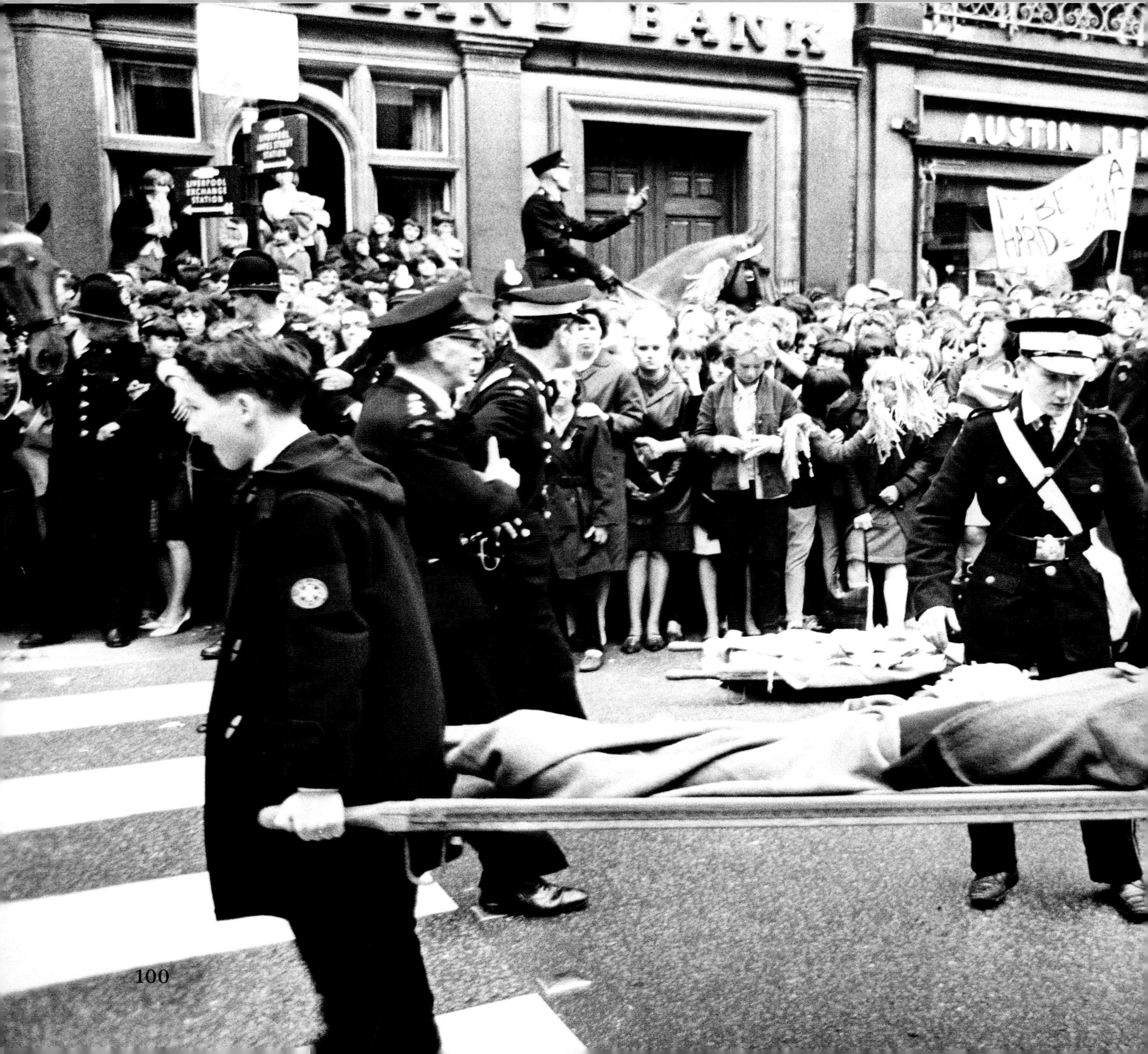
BANK
AUSTIN
LIVERPOOL
EXCHANGE
STATION

◀A fan is carried away on a stretcher, July 10, 1964.

▼Hiding from the fans: walking from Stephenson Place through the passage to the cellar to dodge the crowd before their concert at the Odeon Cinema, New Street Birmingham, October 11, 1964..

101

A HARD DAY'S NIGHT

The album *A Hard Day's Night* was the soundtrack to the eponymous film and was released in June 1964 in the U.S and a month later in the UK. As with the previous albums it was produced by George Martin and released by Parlophone and recorded at the EMI studios in London, but for the first time, also at the Pathé Marconi Studios in Paris. Two hit singles came off the album, the title song—with Paul for once taking the lead vocal—and "Can't Buy Me Love."

There are varying stories as to how the title came about, but the consensus is that it was a malapropism of Ringo's when he was commenting how tired he was after a long working session. All thirteen tracks were written by The Beatles, many of them by John alone, although George wrote "Don't Bother Me." Side one of the LP was the film soundtrack and side two contains unused songs written for the film.

The cover photograph shows five black and white portraits (20 in all) of each of the Fab Four. It was again shot by photographer Robert Freeman who also designed the poster for the film.

Again, Americans did not see the UK version: the songs were packaged differently on *A Hard Day's Night* and *Something New*.

Side 1
1 "A Hard Day's Night"
2 "I Should Have Known Better"
3 "If I Fell"
4 "I'm Happy Just To Dance With You"
5 "And I Love Her"
6 "Tell Me Why"
7 "Can't Buy Me Love"

Side 2
1 "At Any Time At All"
2 "I'll Cry Instead"
3 "Things We Said Today"
4 "When I Get Home"
5 "You Can't Do That"
6 "I'll Be Back"

◀ L–R: George, Pattie, Prudence Bury, Wilfred Brambell, Ringo, and Paul in their special train for the filming of *A Hard Day's Night*, March 5, 1964.

▶ Prudence, George, and Pattie on the train at South Moulton.

The Beatles during filming.

A Hard Day's Night (film)

Director: Richard Lester
Distributor: United Artists
Released: July 1964 (UK),
August 1964 (US)
Black & white. Comedy documentary

Cast:
The Beatles – as themselves
Wilfred Brambell – Paul's grandfather
Victor Spinetti – TV director
Norman Rossington – The Beatles manager

The film shows in madcap comedy style the extraordinary life of The Beatles and was shot at the height of Beatlemania. They wanted to make a comedy rock'n'roll film and chose the best writer and director for their purpose. Rather to the critics' surprise, the film was better than they expected and it proved a big box-office hit. In the long term, it was hugely influential for the way many pop bands were presented to the public and for a number of fast-paced, 1960s comedy/spoof programs as well as for livening up documentary techniques.

Given a budget of £200,000, the filming took just under seven weeks and was shot in black and white to give it the feeling of a documentary.

The screenplay was written by Liverpool-raised Alun Owen who had previously worked with Richard Lester and whose work The Beatles already knew about. He spent a few days with them before starting to write so as to catch their idiom and characters. He came up with a storyline that showed the downside of their fame and the punishing schedules they were required to keep so as not to disappoint their public.

When he had asked them to describe their lives they said it was like "a train and a room and a car and a room and a room and a room." And that pretty much gave him the plot which shows the group catching the train from Liverpool to London where they are to film a TV show. They check in at a hotel then go to the studio. But the long preparations for the production bore Ringo so much that he wanders off for a bit of peace and quiet. When they realize Ringo's missing they go looking for him but can't find him. Ringo

◀ Composer Lionel Bart, Brian Epstein, and Alun Owen at the Cavern, January 1964. Owen wrote the screenplay for *A Hard Day's Night*.

eventually turns up back at the theater after having been arrested with Paul's grandfather. The concert can then go ahead just in the nick of time.

The Beatles themselves had to join the actors union Equity before they could start shooting on the first day at Paddington Station on March 2, 1963. Unusually for a film it was made almost entirely in sequence with much of the filming done around locations in west London with the train sequence shot while traveling between London and Minehead in Somerset. George met his future wife, Pattie Boyd who was working as an extra while making the film.

United Artists liked the film but wanted mid-Atlantic accents dubbed onto them before release in America. The idea was untenable, Paul replied, "Are you kidding? We watch all your cowboy pictures and you go 'Yep' … and we know exactly what you're saying.

"Look, if we can understand a f***ing cowboy talking Texan, they can understand us talking Liverpool." His point was reluctantly accepted.

John, although he liked it, later complained that the film was too one-dimensional

▶Fans crowding the street outside the London Pavilion.

Only a month after the release of *A Hard Day's Night*, The Beatles frantic workload continued when they started recording their fourth album, *Beatles For Sale*, at the EMI Abbey Road studios. The album was targeted for Christmas so had to be recorded and produced quickly so as not to miss out on the top of the festive album charts. Because The Beatles were now so much in demand and their work schedules so tight—they had played in Hong Kong, Australia, New Zealand, Netherlands, Denmark, Sweden, and Britain—by the time they got into the studio to record *Beatles For Sale* they only had two clear weeks to get it done. Again produced by George Martin for Parlophone, it was recorded in various sessions in August, September, and October 1964 and was completed by November 4 and released later that month.

This was the first Beatles album to feature a gatefold cover, and the front was photographed by Robert Freeman. It shows the Fab Four looking more thoughtful—although some have said they were just exhausted. The photo session lasted for a couple of hours and took place in Hyde Park, near the Albert Memorial in central London. There had been no prearrangement about clothes: at the time they all habitually wore the same style of black clothes with white shirts. So without design, the four neatly complement each other.

This album for the first time shows John starting to lose his enthusiasm for the whole Beatlemania phenomenon and penning such questioning songs as "I'm a Loser." The album listed eight new Lennon/McCartney songs plus six covers. In spite of everything, the album stayed in the charts in the UK for 46 weeks and was No.1 for eleven of them.

It was not released in its entirety in the U.S. until 1987; instead Capitol released two albums that

BEATLES FOR SALE

Side 1
1 "No reply"
2 "I'm A Loser"
3 "Baby's In Black"
4 "Rock and Roll Music" (Chuck Berry)
5 "I'll Follow The Sun"
6 "Mr. Moonlight" (Roy Lee Johnson)
7 "Kansas City/Hey-Hey-Hey-Hey!" (Jerry Leiber and Mike Stoller/Richard Penniman)

Side 2
1 "Eight Days a Week"
2 "Words of Love" (Buddy Holly)
3 "Honey Don't" (Carl Perkins)
4 "Every Little Thing"
5 "I Don't Want To Spoil The Party"
6 "What You're Doing"
7 "Everybody's Trying To Be My Baby"
(Carl Perkins)

contained material from *Beatles For Sale—Beatles '65* and *Beatles VI*.

▶ John with a tambourine and a rather tired-looking George Martin.

Released to an eager public on August 6, 1965, *Help!* was the fifth album by The Beatles. Produced as before by George Martin for Parlophone, it forms part of the soundtrack of the eponymous film with seven Beatles' songs on the first side and a further seven that didn't make the movie on the flip side. These latter tracks include Paul's solo performance of his song "Yesterday"—still one of the most covered songs in musical history. The album had 12 Beatles songs, including two by George, as well as two covers.

The U.S. version of *Help!* was very different. It was a soundtrack album including orchestral music. It sold well but The Beatles weren't very happy. Paul said, "But it's a drag, because … We make an album to be like an album, and to be a complete thing." On the other hand, he was happy when "Yesterday"—which wasn't released as a single in the UK—went to No.1 in the US.

Help! was recorded in various sessions at Abbey Road Studios in spring and early summer 1965 and featured an album cover shot by Robert Freeman with the group using semaphore flags. The original idea was to have them signal "HELP" but the proper arrangement did not look artistic enough and instead they spell out NUJV.

◀ Ringo during the filming of *Help!* on Salisbury Plain, May 4, 1965.

HELP!

Side 1
1 "Help !"
2 "The Night Before"
3 "You've Got To Hide Your Love Away"
4 "I Need You"
5 "Another Girl"
6 "You're Going To Lose That Girl"
7 "Ticket To Ride"

Side 2
1 "Act Naturally" (Johnny Russell–Voni Morrison)
2 "It's Only Love"
3 "You Like Me Too Much"
4 "Tell Me What You See"
5 "I've Just Seen A Face"
6 "Yesterday"
7 "Dizzy Miss Lizzy" (Larry Williams)

"No offense, Capitol … but we send it over here and they put the soundtrack on. And, you know, if someone is gonna buy one of our records I think they want to hear us and not soundtrack."

Paul McCartney

111

This scene was shot at the "City Barge" pub,
Strand-on-the-Green Kew, April 24, 1965.

Help! (film)

Director: Richard Lester
Distributor: United Artists/Apple Fuilms
Released: July 1965 (UK),
August 1965 (US)
Color. Comedy drama

Cast:

The Beatles – as themselves
Leo McKern – Swami Clang
Eleanor Bron – High Priestess Ahme
Victor Spinetti – Foot
Roy Kinnear – Algernon

With a bigger budget thanks to the success of *A Hard Day's Night*, this time a couple of exotic locations were used—Switzerland and the Bahamas—as well as England. Directed by Dick Lester and originally titled "Eight Arms to Hold You," the basic plot concerns a big ring sent to Ringo from a fan, but when he puts it on he cannot get it off. It turns out that whoever wears the ring has to be sacrificed to Kali. The film turns into a chase and hide adventure with the Kali cult members trying to sacrifice Ringo while the other Beatles try to save him. To make matters worse, the Chief Inspector at Scotland Yard is chasing them all and a couple of mad scientists are also attempting to secure the ring for themselves.

The Beatles themselves were not very clear about the script but were happy and relaxed during filming, during which they all confessed to smoking a lot of pot. Despite Lester's relaxed attitude with The Beatles, the filming schedule was very tight, so much so that he was editing completed scenes at night before shooting again the next day.

It was filmed partially in Switzerland because The Beatles requested a skiing holiday; in fact none of them had ever skied before and George swore after that he never would again. Paul, however, enjoyed skiing so much that he soon returned for a holiday. Unfortunately, much of the extra footage and out-takes have been destroyed or lost as at that time The Beatles were not expected to last as a phenomenon and no great care was taken of the unused film.

Throughout the making of *Help!* Paul was continuously humming as he struggled with a new melody … hugely irritating in particular Lester. Called "Scrambled Eggs" the song finally appeared

◄ Royal premiere of *Help!* at the London Pavilion, July 29, 1965.

as "Yesterday." The other milestone during filming was that George discovered the sitar and the Indian music which would so influence his musical style and lifestyle.

"Help! relegates the group to the sidelines for long stretches, or as Lennon pointed out sourly, the Beatles were made extras in their own movie.*"*

▼ Shooting *Help!* on Salisbury Plain at Knighton Down, May 3, 1965.

Tim Brayton

115

RUBBER SOUL

Rubber Soul was recorded at the EMI Studios in London between June 17 and November 11, 1965, with the intention of being released in time for sales at Christmas. By this time The Beatles were undeniably the biggest band in the world and as a consequence were allowed complete creative control—a very unusual concession from the record company.

Produced by George Martin—who summed up the making of the album as being "a very joyful time"—it was their sixth album and featured 14 original songs that introduced fans to their increasing musical sophistication and moved away from regular pop songs. Furthermore, their manager Brian Epstein, was completely hands-off letting them go their own way musically, unlike Capitol in the US whose selection of tracks completely changed the feel of the album.

The songs were more introspective, Paul later remarked that they all thought, "Now we can branch out into songs that are more surreal, a little more entertaining." They also later admitted that these more mellow sounds were influenced by their collective use of marijuana.

A distinctive element of this album is the use of unusual instruments and sounds. Whenever they lacked inspiration, they had a root around in the instrument cupboard that contained a plethora of strange equipment such as Moroccan drums and strange tambourines. In particular, George used a sitar on "Norwegian Wood" after become entranced by the instrument while in India.

The album cover photograph was again taken by Robert Freeman (it would his last for the band) at John's house and this particular shot was chosen collectively by the group for its unusual angle. By this time they were so well-known that they didn't need to have the band name on the cover. The US album came

Side 1
1 "Drive My Car"
2 "Norwegian Wood"
3 "You Won't See Me"
4 "Nowhere Man"
5 "Think For Yourself"
6 "The Word"
7 "Michelle"

Side 2
1 "What Goes On"
2 "Girl"
3 "I'm Looking Through You"
4 "In My Life"
5 "Wait"
6 "If I Needed Someone"
7 "Run For Your Life"

"... it's also one of rock's first album-qua-albums; not a raft for a few hits or a soundtrack to a wacky film, but something to be listened to and contemplated from start to finish."

Josh Tyrangiel (TIME entertainment)

out three days later than the UK release and contained a different, more folky, selection of tracks as well as some different recordings of the same tracks. Capitol's choice of material worked for the US: it went to No.1 and was well-received by press and public alike.

Rubber Soul was released in December 1965 and topped the UK album charts for eight weeks. It was and still is regarded with great affection, with *Rolling Stone* saying it "achieved a new musical sophistication and a greater thematic depth".

For George this was the best album they made, "Everything was blossoming at that time, including us, because we were still growing."

▲ *Rubber Soul* cover.

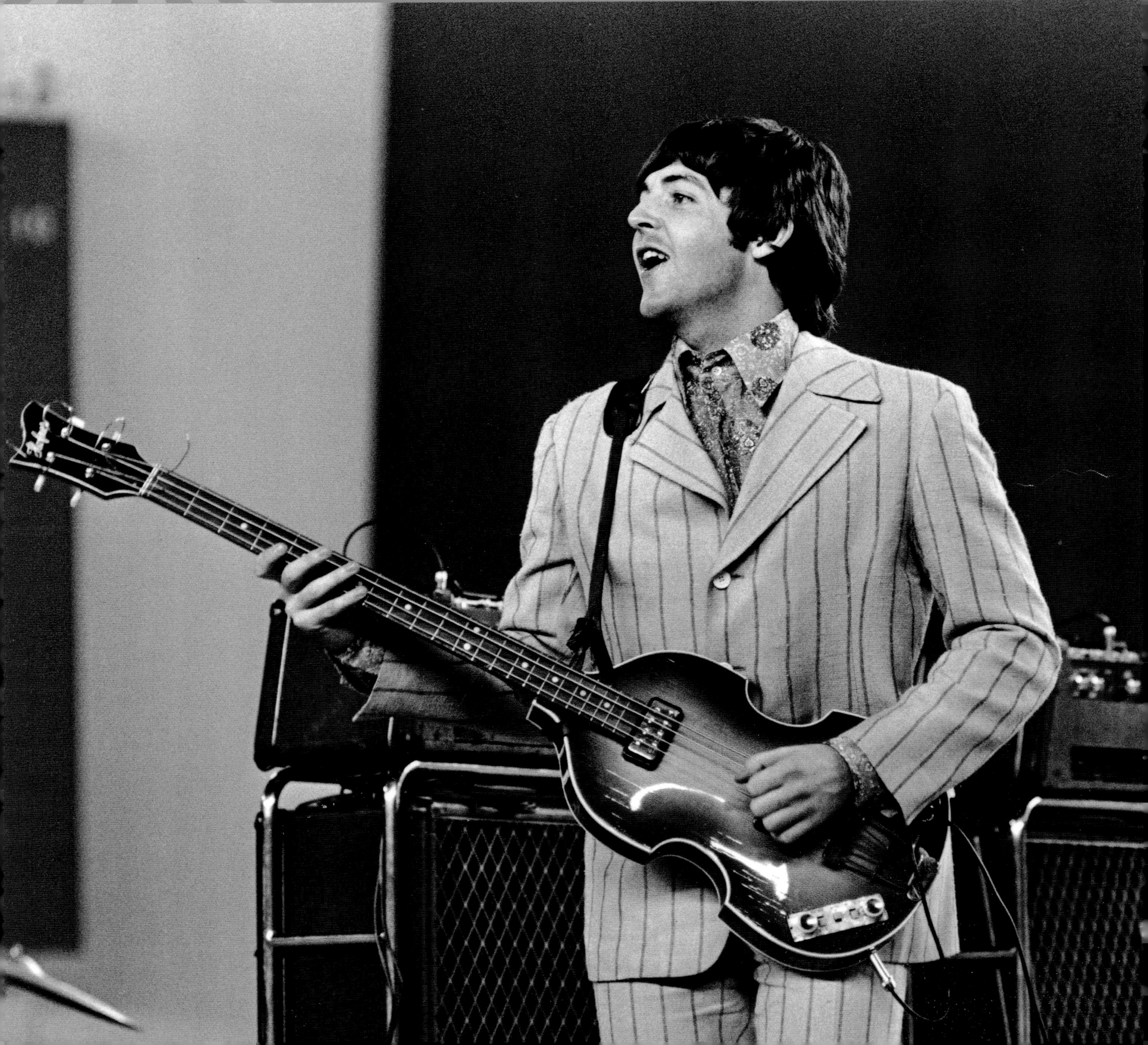

LIFE AT THE TOP
1966

“They were doing things nobody was doing. Their chords were outrageous, just outrageous, and their harmonies made it all valid. Everybody else thought they were for the teenyboppers, that they were gonna pass right away. But it was obvious to me that they had staying power. I knew they were pointing to the direction where music had to go.”

Bob Dylan

◄ Paul on stage during the last tour.

Timeline

1966

January 8—*Rubber Soul* tops the *Billboard* album chart for the first of six weeks. "We Can Work It Out" is at No.1 on the singles chart.

January 21—George marries Pattie Boyd at the Leatherhead and Esher Register Office; Paul and Brian are best men. John and Ringo are on holiday in Trinidad.

February 8—George and Pattie fly to Barbados for their honeymoon.

February 15—Capitol release "Nowhere Man"/"What Goes On," which reaches No.3 on the *Billboard* chart. It still sells well enough to be certified gold on April 1.

February 28—The Cavern closes with debts of £10,000.

March 1—*The Beatles At Shea Stadium* premieres on BBC TV in black and white.

March 4—Parlophone releases the EP "Yesterday" which will reach No.1 on March 26.
John Lennon's interview with Maureen Cleave appears in the *Evening Standard*. His comments on Christianity will lead to hysteria in the US.

March 15—they receive ten nominations for the Grammys, but win nothing.

► George and Pattie sign the register at Epsom Registry Office, January 21, 1966.

► The controversial "Butcher" cover of *The Beatles Yesterday and Today* was released on June 14, 1966.

March 24—all four Beatles attend the premiere of the film *Alfie*, in which Jane Asher had a role, at the Haymarket Theatre in London.

March 25—Robert Whitaker takes the "butcher" photographs that will become controversial when one is used on the cover of *The Beatles Yesterday and Today*.

April 1—Paul and John visit the Indica Gallery—which Paul helped finance and where in 1966 John will meet Yoko Ono—and John buys Timothy Leary's LSD manual

The Psychedelic Experience: A Manual Based On The Tibetan Book Of The Dead.

April 6–June 22—the band records and mixes *Revolver*.

May 1—the band play the *NME* Pollwinners Concert at the Empire Pool, Wembley, which is—until their Abbey Road rooftop session—their last ever British concert. They play five songs and the program airs on May 15.

May 26—The Beatles all meet and spend time with their friend Bob

▶ Press conference before the Harrisons flew off to Barbados for their honeymoon.

Dylan while he is in London. He visits Kenwood after his first show at the Royal Albert Hall.

May 27—John and Dylan are filmed by D.A. Pennebaker (who produced *Dont Look Back*, the film of Dylan's 1965 tour) driving to Dylan's hotel for an ABC program that does not air. John and George later go to Dylan's concert at the Royal Albert Hall.

May 30—Capitol releases "Paperback Writer"/"Rain," another million+ seller that spends two weeks at No.1 and is certified gold on July 14.

June 10—Parlophone release "Paperback Writer"/"Rain" and it reaches No.1 a week later.

June 15—Capitol release, *The Beatles Yesterday and Today* but withdraw it immediately because of complaints about the so-called "Butcher" cover. They paste another Whitaker image over the image and re-release on June 20.

June 16—The Beatles make their only live appearance on BBC TV's *Top of the Pops* performing "Paperback Writer" and "Rain."

June 17—Paul buys High Park

▶ George and Pattie in Barbados on Valentine's Day during their honeymoon.

▶Press conference on the final German tour.

▼Onstage, at Hamburg's Ernst Mencken Halle June 26, 1966.

▼▶On stage at Munich's Circus Krone Bau, June 24, 1966.

Farm (all 183 acres of it) near Cambeltown, Kintyre, in Scotland.
June 23–27—The Beatles fly to Munich on the 23rd and play there on the 24th, in Essen (25th), and Hamburg (26th), before returning to the UK. They meet Astrid Kirchherr and Bert Kaempfert while in Hamburg.
June 27—The Beatles fly back to London and then leave for Tokyo, but have to divert to Anchorage because of bad weather.
June 30—they arrive in Tokyo and

play the first of five sets in front of small audiences at the Budokan Hall. They then play two sets each on July 1 and 2.

July 3—if anything confirmed The Beatles' desire to stop touring it was their visit to the Philippines. They flew to Manila via Hong Kong and played two football stadium shows (in front of 30,000 and 50,000 fans) the following day. But poor organization meant they missed an engagement with Imelda, the wife of dictator Ferdinand Marcos. Flying out of the Philippines they and their crew were badly treated—particularly Mal and chauffeur Alf Bicknell—and were robbed of the proceeds by a phony tax bill.

July 6–7—a stop off in Delhi on their way home to London. George buys a sitar. They leave India on an evening flight.

July 8—Parlophone releases the *Nowhere Man* EP with four tracks from *Rubber Soul*. It reaches No.4.

July 12—The Beatles win three 1965 Ivor Novello awards: "Yesterday" is the most outstanding song of the year; "We Can Work It Out" the top-selling song; and *Help!* is the second-best selling album.

July 30—US teen magazine *Datebook* republishes John's "more

PHILIPPINES
Beatles clash with President. Beatles row with Taxmen.

popular than Jesus" quote and US fundamentalists reacted by burning Beatles' books and records..

July 30—*Yesterday ... And Today* reaches No.1 on the *Billboard* album chart. It will stay there for five weeks and to date has sold over two million copies.

▲ A Franklin cartoon published July 6, 1966, after the Philippines furore. Ringo: "I thought it was the usual police escort."

◀ Taking the train, during a tour of Europe, June 22, 1966.

" And so they started knocking over our road managers and things, and everyone was falling all over the place. *"*

Paul McCartney

> "Christianity will go. It will vanish and shrink. I needn't argue about that; I'm right and I'll be proved right. We're more popular than Jesus now; I don't know which will go first—rock 'n' roll or Christianity."

John Lennon

July 31—in Birmingham, AL, as a reaction to *Datebook*'s article, they make a bonfire of Beatles' records and memorabilia.

August 5—Parlophone releases "Yellow Submarine"/"Eleanor Rigby" and it reaches No.1 on August 20, spending four weeks on top.

With a brilliant cover by Klaus Voormann, *Revolver* is also released to huge critical applause. Advance sales of over 300,000 propel it to No.1 where it stays for seven weeks.

August 8—Capitol releases "Yellow Submarine"/"Eleanor Rigby" but Southern States ban its sales because of the "more popular than Jesus" furore and it only reaches No.2 on the *Billboard* chart.

The issue doesn't seem to affect sales of *Revolver*, also released (minus three songs) on the 8th. It spends six weeks at the top and will later be voted third in *Rolling Stone's* top 500 albums.

In South Africa, Beatles' records are banned as irreligious by the apartheid regime.

August 12–29—the third and final US tour starts in Chicago in front of 13,000; 30,000 watch them in Detroit on the 13th, the day that the Klu Klux Klan parade around a book-burning pyre; 20,000 are at Cleveland; 32,000 in D.C., 21,000 in Philadelphia, 32,000 in Toronto (where John makes things worse by coming out on the side of the Vietnam draft dodgers), 25,000 in Boston, 22,500 in Memphis, 23,000 in St. Louis, 13,000 in

Cincinnati, 44,000 in New York, 22,500 in Seattle, 45,000 in LA, and finally, 22,500 as their final touring concert takes place at Candlestick Park, San Francisco.

September 5—John, accompanied by Neil Aspinall, flies to Hannover to begin filming *How I Won The War* directed by Richard Lester, who did *A Hard Day's Night*. John starts wearing his trademark granny glasses and writes "Strawberry Fields" during the filming, which continues (after a weekend in Paris with Paul and Brian) in Spain. Ringo and Maureen join him on October 4.

▶ Press conference at Heathrow after the return from Manila, July 8.

▼ Brian and the band arrive back at Heathrow.

September 14—George and Pattie fly to India where George is to take sitar lessons from Ravi Shankar; they stay at the Taj Mahal Hotel in Bombay and return to London on October 22.

September 26—Brian overdoses and ends up in the Priory: he will spend a lot of time there until his death.

November 9—John meets Yoko Ono at "Unfinished paintings and Objects" at the Indica Gallery and is knocked out by her and her art.

November 24—first day of recording for the new album (*Sgt. Pepper*) which will be released in May next year.

November 27—John makes an appearance in Peter Cook and Dudley Moore's *Not Only. . . But Also* TV series.

December 9—Parlophone releases *A Collection Of Beatles Oldies* which reaches No.7.

December 18—launch of *The Family Way*, a film directed by Ray Boulting featuring a soundtrack mainly composed by Paul and scored by him and George Martin. The soundtrack was released by Decca in the name of the George Martin Orchestra, on January 6. It won a Ivor Novello Award in 1967.

◀ ▲ ▶ November 1—the first day of recording for *Sgt. Pepper*: the band members make their way into the Abbey Road studios.

29

stereo

REVOLVER

The band, with George Martin at the Abbey Road Studios, produced their seventh album and for many fans, their greatest. This was their first recorded exploration of psychedelic rock and took them to the No.1 album slot around the world. Of the 14 tracks, three are penned by George, the rest by Paul and John.

Recorded between early April and late June it includes the seminal song "Eleanor Rigby" (which was released as a double A-side with "Yellow Submarine"). For this album there was much more experimental music and playing around with double-tracking, running the tapes backwards, and unusual noises and instruments. George Martin remembered that for *Revolver* The Beatles were much more assertive and interested in following their own ideas and exploring the potential of different recording techniques. John later remarked that "*Rubber Soul* was the pot album and *Revolver* was the acid."

For the album cover they approached their old Hamburg friend and artist Klaus Voormann, who added collage photographs taken by another old friend, Robert Whitaker. They were very pleased with the result and rather flattered by the portraits. The title *Revolver* was only decided after long debate only a month before its release. It has a double meaning: a revolver being, of course, a gun, but also the way a record revolves on a turntable. *Revolver* frequently tops lists of greatest album of all time.

◀ Klaus Voormann designed the album cover for *Revolver*.

REVOLVER

Side 1
1 "Taxman"
2 "Eleanor Rigby"
3 "I'm Only Sleeping"
4 "Love You To"
5 "Here, There and Everywhere"
6 "Yellow Submarine"
7 "She Said, She Said"

Side 2
1 "Good Day Sunshine"
2 "And Your Bird Can Sing"
3 "For No One"
4 "Dr. Robert"
5 "I Want To Tell You"
6 "Got To Get You Into My Life"
7 "Tomorrow Never Knows"

“We were having more fun in the studio … it was getting more experimental, the songs were getting better, more interesting.”

Ringo Starr

131

The Beatles and America

When Pan Am Flight 101 landed at JFK Airport on February 7, 1964, at around 1:20pm bringing The Beatles to America, most people didn't know what to expect. They were only booked for a handful of concerts and a couple of TV appearances. However, they did have the No.1 single with "I Want To Hold Your Hand," rush-released by Capitol Records, EMI's US subsidiary. For a long time, Capitol had not been interested in The Beatles: that would all change. However, as in the UK, they were greeted by screaming fans: some 3,000 turned up.

Two days later they performed live on *The Ed Sullivan Show* to an estimated 74 million viewers, almost half the U.S. population. Many of the critics scoffed that they would amount to nothing. But the next day at the Washington Coliseum they triumphed.

▲ The band poses for a group photo on a day off in Miami during their 1964 tour.
▶ The ground-breaking first live performance on CBS's *The Ed Sullivan Show*, February 9, 1964.

> ❝The Beatles are not merely awful. They are so unbelievably horrible, so appallingly unmusical, so dogmatically insensitive to the magic of the art, that they qualify as crowned heads of anti-music.❞
>
> *William F. Buckley* (US conservative commentator)

After another appearance on *The Ed Sullivan Show* they flew back to England. By April they held the top five *Billboard* Hot 100 spots plus another seven positions on the chart. Their three albums also topped the US charts.

The following August they returned to the US and full-throttle Beatlemania—and a grueling 30-concert, 23-city tour. This time they could dictate terms: they would not perform in front of segregated audiences. Each gig lasted a frenetic 30 minutes, but because of the high-pitched screaming nobody could hear any of the music.

The third American tour started on August 15, 1965, with a sell-out concert at Shea Stadium in front of 55,600 near-hysterical fans and 2,000 security

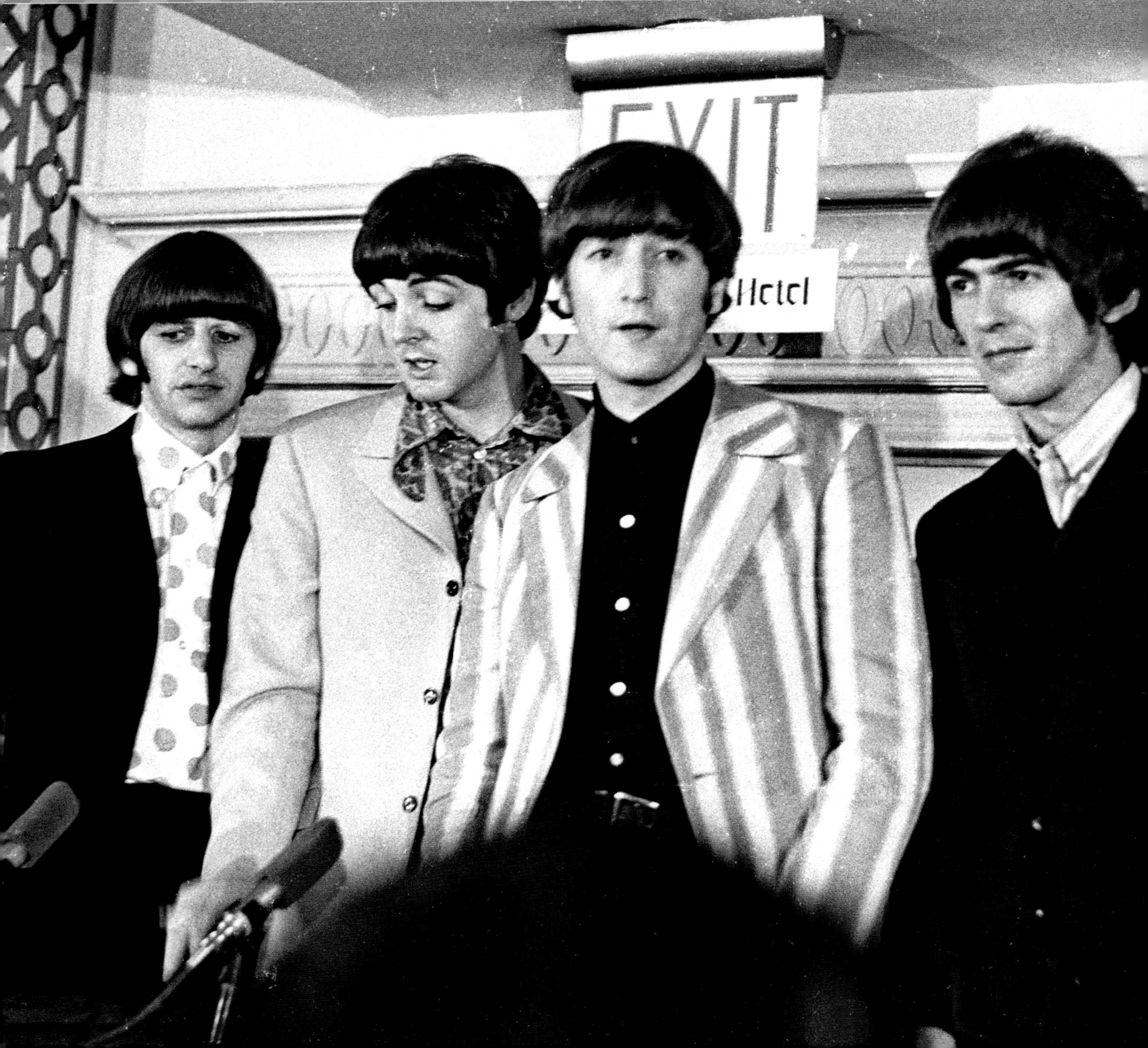
EXIT

personnel. This was followed by another nine concerts, including two at the Hollywood Bowl.

In March 1966 in a passing remark that appeared in the *Evening Standard*, John observed that they were "more popular than Jesus." There was little reaction in Britain, but five months later across the Atlantic when it was repeated in *Datebook* magazine, there was a radical reaction. Brian and John apologized but to no avail: their lives were threatened, and in some states their music was banned, their records burned, and there were anti-Beatle demonstrations. For their fourth tour the atmosphere had turned toxic … but still the fans turned out in droves to watch them. It started on August 12, 1966, with the first gig in Chicago and their last was at Candlestick Park, San Francisco, their last ever.

However, in spite of the furore, The Beatles' popularity in the US was huge and certainly responsible for the bulk of their sales. The country took the band to its heart, and they still retain an enormous fan base in America.

▲ Poster for the final concert at Candlestick Park.

◀ Press conference following the Shea Stadium concert, August 23, 1965.

▼ Damage limitation: John apologies for "more popular than Jesus," August 16, 1966.

"The thing is, Capitol issue all sort of mad stuff, you know. It's nothing to do with us. We take 14 tracks to be put out, but they keep a couple and put them out later."

George Harrison

135

PSYCHEDELIA
1967-68

"Strawberry Fields is a real place ... a house near a boys' reformatory where I used to go to garden parties as a kid with my friends Nigel and Pete."

John Lennon (Playboy, 1980)

◄ The Beatles and their wives at the film premiere of *How I Won the War*.

Timeline

1967

January 15—Paul and George see Donovan in concert and George gives Donovan sitar lessons a few days later. Donovan was a friend—he dated Pattie Boyd's sister and would go to India with the band. Paul later said Donovan had taught John and him some finger-picking guitar techniques.

January 11—Paul sees and is impressed by David Mason's trumpet playing on TV. He's quickly booked to record the "Penny Lane" trumpet solo and goes on to be involved in other songs on *Sgt.*

▼ Ringo, Maureen, and first son Zak.

Pepper, Magical Mystery Tour, and "All You Need Is Love."

January 27—Brian Epstein and the Beatles sign a new record deal with EMI. The extra control ensures that Capitol will not be able to change the content of their records in future. The company reveal that the group has sold 180 million records in less than five years.

January 29—John and Paul go to see Jimi Hendrix, who is supporting The Who, in concert at the Saville Theatre.

January 31—Under pressure from EMI Brian Epstein asks George Martin for a new single. Martin hands over "Penny Lane" and "Strawberry Fields Forever."

February 13—Capitol releases "Penny Lane"/"Strawberry Fields Forever." Goes gold on March 20 but only stays at No.1 for a week.

February 17—Parlophone releases "Penny Lane"/"Strawberry Fields Forever." One of the greatest singles ever only reaches No.2.

February 19—John and Ringo see Chuck Berry and Del Shannon in concert at the Saville Theatre.

March 2—three Grammys go to the band: Paul wins a Best Contemporary (R&R) Solo Vocal Performance—Male for "Eleanor

Rigby"; "Michelle" is Song Of The Year and *Revolver* is honored for best cover artwork.

March 25—The Beatles receive three Ivor Novello awards: for "Michelle" (most broadcast song, 1966), "Yellow Submarine" (top-selling record, 1966), and "Yesterday" is runner-up in the "most performed" section.

March 30—the brilliant living collage of Beatles' heroes for the cover of *Sgt. Pepper*, designed by Peter Blake and his wife Jann Haworth, is photographed by Michael Cooper in Blake's Chelsea studio.

April 1–12—Paul, traveling with Mal Evans, flies to Denver to surprise Jane Asher on her 21st birthday. She is on tour performing in *Romeo and Juliet*. Near the end of his trip, Paul devises the *Magical Mystery Tour* idea and develops it with Mal on the flight home.

April 10—While in Los Angeles Paul visits Beach Boys' Brian Wilson who was recording for his *Smile* project.

April 24—all four Beatles go to Donovan's opening night of his week at the Saville Theatre.

April 25—work begins on *Magical Mystery Tour.*

▶John Lennon's psychedelically painted Rolls-Royce leaves the car paint shop of J.P. Fallon May 25, 1967.

April 29—John visits a benefit for the *International Times*—the 14 Hour Technicolor Dream—at Alexandra Palace. Among the performers is Yoko Ono.

May 12—Radio London, the pirate ship in the North Sea, plays the whole of *Sgt Pepper's Lonely Hearts Club Band*: other stations—particularly in the US—have been playing individual tracks.

May 15—Paul goes to the Bag O' Nails club to see Georgie Fame and meets Linda Eastman. He'll meet her again on the 19th when she takes photos at *Sgt. Pepper*'s launch party.

May 18—John and Paul sing backing vocals on the Rolling Stones' "We Love You" single, to show solidarity with the three Stones who are being prosecuted for possession of drugs.

May 19—Brian Epstein hosts a press party for the launch of *Sgt Pepper* at his 24 Chapel Street house in Belgravia. He'll also have a private party at his house in Surrey on May 28.

May 20—BBC radio plays most of *Sgt Pepper* on *Where It's At*—but it omits "A Day in The Life," which it has banned for drug referencces.

▲Maureen leaves hospital with newborn Jason, August 1967.

May 24—The Beatles see Procol Harum at the Speakeasy.

June 1—Parlophone releases *Sgt Pepper's Lonely Hearts Club Band* to universal acclaim ... which continues to this day. It was rated No.1 in Rolling Stone's 500 Greatest Albums. With advance orders around 250,000 copies, between 1967 and 1976 it spent 148 weeks on the charts, 27 at No.1. To date sales are over 32 million copies.

June 2—the next day Capitol releases *Sgt Pepper* in the US to similar plaudits. It will spend 175 weeks on the charts, 15 at

No.1 and to date has sold over 11 million copies in the US—certifying diamond on January 10, 1997.

June 4—Paul is among the audience at the Saville Theatre where the Jimi Hendrix Experience perform the title track to *Sgt Pepper's Lonely Hearts Club Band* to open their set.

June 8—Brian Jones is invited to a session at Abbey Road by Paul. Brian plays the sax solo on "You Know My Name (Look Up My Number)."

June 14–26—the band records and mixes "All You Need Is Love" commissioned for *Our World* (see below).

June 25—The Beatles segment of the *Our World* international TV program is broadcast live from Abbey Road to an audience of some 400 million worldwide. The Beatles represent the UK and perform "All You Need Is Love."

July 3—John, Paul and George, with Cynthia, Pattie and Jane attend a private party for the Monkees. Also present, Eric Clapton who will fall for Pattie.

July 7—"All You Need Is Love"/"Baby You're A Rich Man" released by Parlophone. No.1 from July 22, it spends three weeks at the top.

July 17—"All You Need Is

▶The Beatles prepare for the *"Our World"* TV broadcast, June 25, 1967.

Love"/"Baby You're A Rich Man" released by Capitol also goes to No.1.

July 21—John's idea, enthusiastically endorsed by Magic Alex, of The Beatles and their friends living together on an island has them heading for Greece, except Maureen who is heavily pregnant. By the end of the month they had all flown home and the idea was dead.

July 24—Paul funds, and Brian and all four Beatles sign, a full-page advert in *The Times* calling for the legalization of marijuana.

August 1–9—George and Pattie fly to LA where they rent a house on Blue Jay Way. During the trip, George spends much time with

> ❝A dream you dream alone is only a dream. A dream you dream together is reality.❞
>
> *Yoko Ono*

◀ The Beatles with the Maharishi Mahesh Yogi, August 1967.

Ravi Shankar and takes more sitar lessons.

August 19—Ringo and Maureen's second son, Jason, is born.

August 24—John, Cynthia, Paul, Jane, George, and Pattie attend the Maharishi Mahesh Yogi's lecture at the Hilton Hotel in London.

August 25—John, Paul, Jane, Ringo, George, and Pattie leave London with the Maharishi for North Wales where they are to attend his lectures at a college in Bangor.

August 27—Brian Epstein is found dead at home in Chapel Street. He has overdosed on Carbitral sleeping pills. The Beatles leave Wales to return to London. There is a family funeral on August 29.

September 1—the band and Tony Barrow meet to discuss the future in light of Brian's death and decide to continue *Magical Mystery Tour*.

September 11–24—the bulk of the filming for *Magical Mystery Tour*. After leaving London and picking up John, George and Ringo in Surrey, the first port of call was Teignmouth in the West of England; the last, West Malling in Sussex.

October 17—The Beatles attend Brian Epstein's memorial service at the New London Synagogue.

October 18—all four Beatles, their wives and girlfriends, attend the premiere of *How I Won The War* in London.

November 1—The last day of filming for *Magical Mystery Tour* ... followed on the 7th by the last day of recording.

November 17—The Beatles Ltd. becomes Apple Music Ltd.

November 22—George starts work on his *Wonderwall* film soundtrack.

November 24—Parlophone release "Hello Goodbye"/"I Am The Walrus" which reaches No.1 on December 9. It will spend seven weeks there. Unfortunately, the BBC take exception to the use of

▲ Launching *How I Won The War*. John and director Richard Lester.

"The first line was written on one acid trip one weekend. The second line was written on the next acid trip the next weekend."

John Lennon talking about "I am the Walrus" (Playboy, 1980)

◀▲John, Cynthia, George, Pattie and her sister "Jenny" at Heathrow Airport ready to fly off to India, February 1968.

the word "knickers" and bans "I Am The Walrus."

November 27—Capitol releases "Hello Goodbye"/"I Am The Walrus" as a single (it reaches No.1 on December 30) and *Magical Mystery Tour* as an LP. The LP sells 1.5 million in a month, is certified gold on December 15 and spends 91 weeks in the charts, eight of them at No.1. So good is the reception, that EMI import copies back to the UK and it is this rather than the EP that becomes a CD in 1987.

December 3–8—Ringo works on the movie *Candy* in Rome.

Paul takes Jane to his Scottish farmhouse on holiday.

December 5—the Apple Boutique opening party at 94 Baker Street ... is followed on the 7th by its opening to the public. It is a massive financial mistake, and folds on July 31, 1968.

December 8—Parlophone releases *Magical Mystery Tour* as an EP. It sells half a million in a month and reaches No.2 on the singles chart (the EP chart had just been discontinued) kept off the top by "Hello Goodbye."

December 25—Paul and Jane

announce their engagement: after four years together it was tempting fate, and by July 20 it's all over.

December 26—*Magical Mystery Tour* premieres on BBC TV, in black and white, to 20 million viewers: the critics don't like it. It repeats in color on January 5.

1968

January 7—George and Neil Aspinall fly to India to work with local musicians on his *Wonderwall* film soundtrack at EMI Bombay.

January 17—The Beatles minus George, who was still away, went to a reception for Grapefruit, a band managed by Apple who had signed to RCA.

January 22—Apple Corp. opens offices in London.

January 25—the band travels to Twickenham Film Studios to film their appearance at the end of *Yellow Submarine*.

February 6—Ringo appears on Cilla Black's TV show for which Paul has supplied the theme song, "Step Inside Love."

February 8—Comedian Spike Milligan, who George Martin had produced, watched the Beatles recording "Across The Universe" and they agreed he could use the song as the theme for a World

▼The Beatles and their wives at Rishikesh with the Maharishi. On the dais, L–R: Ringo, Maureen, Jane, Paul, George, Pattie, Cynthia, John. Next to John is Mal Evans and Beach Boy Mike Love.

◄ Paul with Apple Records new signing Mary Hopkin.

leave Rishikesh: Ringo's delicate stomach and being away from their children proved too much.

March 9—*Sgt. Pepper* wins four Grammys: Album of the Year, Best Contemporary Album, Best Album Cover, Best Engineered Recording, Non-Classical.

March 15—Parlophone releases "Lady Madonna"/"The Inner Light." It reaches No.1 on March 30 and spends two weeks there.

March 18—The Beatles last release by Capitol, "Lady Madonna"/"The Inner Light," only reaches No.4 but sells over a million copies in the first week and on February 17, 1999, is certified platinum.

March 26—Neil Aspinall, Paul, and Jane returned to London from Rishikesh. Paul and Jane head for the farm in Scotland. Magic Alex heads out to India.

The Beatles win three Ivor Novello awards: "Hey Jude" A-Side With the Highest Sales; "She's Leaving Home" Best Song of 1967; "Hello Goodbye" the second best-selling.

April 12—John, Cynthia, George and Pattie leave Rishikesh, because, it is said, the Maharishi made overtures to the girls. John

Wildlife Charity album he was involved with.

February 16—John, Cynthia, George, Pattie and her sister "Jenny" fly to Delhi. Mal Evans preceded them: he took on their luggage and arranged transport (taxis) to take them to Rishikesh. Mia Farrow joins them at Delhi and three days later, Paul, Jane, Ringo, and Maureen follow on.

February 29—Yoko leaves her husband and contacts John.

March 1—Ringo and Maureen

writes "Sexy Sadie" about him at the airport. George and Pattie go to Madras to see Ravi Shankar.

May 5—Twiggy sees Mary Hopkin on *Opportunity Knocks*, and suggests to Paul that Apple sign her.

May 11–15—John, Paul, and Neil Aspinall fly to New York to launch Apple Corp Ltd. in America. Paul meets Linda Eastman again.

May 15—George, Pattie, Ringo, and Maureen go to Cannes for the premiere of *Wonderwall* as Paul and John fly home from New York.

May 19—John and Yoko Ono's relationship starts while Cynthia is in Greece. At Kenwood they record experimental sounds.

May 23—Apple Tailoring opens at 161 Kings Road.

May 30—work began on the material written in India that will form the basis of *The Beatles* double album. Recording will finish on October 17.

June 7—George and Ringo along with their wives flew to Los Angeles so that George could appear in a documentary about Ravi Shankar. They return on the 18th.

June 8—Paul was best man at his brother Mike's wedding.

June 15—John and Yoko appeared in public as a couple for the first time planting an acorn for peace at St. Michael's Cathedral, Coventry;

three days later they are at the opening of the National Theatre production of *In His Own Write* directed by Victor Spinetti.

June 20—Paul flies to the US, attends a meeting with Capitol in Los Angeles on the 22nd, where he is joined by Linda Eastman, and returns to London on the 25th.

June 30—Paul records the Black Dyke Mills Band in Saltaire near Bradford, performing one of his compositions. It will be released on Apple.

July 1—Opening of John and Yoko's "You Are Here" exhibition at which John publicly declares his

▲ Paul records with the Black Dyke Mill brass band, Saltaire, Yorkshire, June 30, 1968. His old English sheepdog Martha is at his side.

love for Yoko.

July 17—Geoff Emerick, their long-time engineer, quits because of the bickering; he's not the only one. Ringo quits in August and George goes away to Greece to get away from it all.

July 8—the premiere of *Yellow Submarine* at the London Pavilion in Piccadilly. The Beatles had had little involvement and were pleasantly surprised by the outcome.

◄John and the pregnant Yoko leave Marylebone Magistates Court, October 18, 1968.

July 20—Jane Asher announces on *The Simon Dee Show* her engagement to Paul is off.

July 28—the "Mad Day Out" sees war photographer Don McCullin photograph the band in various locations around London.

July 29—Work starts on "Hey Jude."

July 31—The Beatles close their unsuccessful Apple Boutique, giving everything away to passers-by.

August 8—John and Paul attend Mick Jagger's 25th birthday party.

August 11—Apple Music is launched.

August 22—Cynthia sues John for divorce.

August 26—Apple releases "Hey Jude"/"Revolution" on Capitol in the US and, in spite of its seven-minutes length, is hugely successful. It spends nine weeks at No.1, is certified gold on September 13, and platinum in February 1999.

August 30—Apple releases "Hey Jude"/"Revolution" in the UK. It spends two weeks on top of the

◄John, Yoko, and Peter Brown after John was fined for cannabis possession, November 28, 1968.

charts from September 14.

September 9—George Martin is the next to feel the pressure and leaves the in-fighting; he goes away till October 1.

September 30—Hunter Davies' classic book *The Beatles* is published. It is the only authorized biography to date.

October 18—John and Yoko are busted. They appear before the magistrate at Marylebone and are remanded on bail. Yoko is pregnant, a fact made public on October 25.

October 31—Linda Eastman moves to Paul's London flat with her daughter Heather. She had spent most of the last month with Paul and they had then spent ten days in New York after *The Beatles* had been completed.

November 1—George Harrison releases *Wonderwall Music*, the first Beatles solo album and first on Apple. Although he doesn't play on it, George writes and produces the album. It is released in the US on December 2.

November 4—the stress gets to Yoko and she's admitted to hospital. She miscarries later in the month.

November 8—Cynthia and John are divorced.

November 11—*Unfinished Music*

No 1: Two Virgins by John Lennon and Yoko Ono is released by Apple in the US. It is an "avant-garde" album with a cover that shows the pair naked. Few stores will take it; copies are seized by customs for being indecent but it still manages to get onto the US charts.

November 22— Apple releases *The Beatles* (aka *The White Album*) in the UK. It is a huge success, with advance orders of more than 250,000. It enters the charts on December 1 at No.1. It will spend 24 weeks on the charts, eight of them at the top.

November 25—US release of *The Beatles* on Capitol. It takes three weeks to reach No.1, stays there for nine weeks, and spends 155 weeks in the top 200. It will become the tenth best-selling album in the US.

November 28—John pleads guilty to possession of cannabis, taking sole responsibility. He is found guilty and fined. This conviction will cause problems in the future when he tries to get a green card to stay in the US.

November 29—John and Yoko's *Two Virgins* album is released in the UK.

December 9—*Newsweek* reports that after only five days on sale, *The Beatles* has sold 1.1 million copies in America.

December 10—John and Yoko attend rehearsals for the Rolling Stones *Rock and Roll Circus*, filming the program the following day. John plays "Yer Blues" with Clapton, Keith Richards, and Hendrix's drummer Mitch Mitchell, after which they back Yoko and violinist Ivry Gitlis. The project does not get shown until 1995.

December 17—*Magical Mystery Tour* film opens in the US.

December 23—John and Yoko were Father and Mother Christmas at the Apple Christmas party at 3 Savile Row.

> "I haven't broken it off, but it is broken off, finished."
>
> *Jane Asher*

▼The Rolling Stones Rock 'n' Roll Circus—Pete Townshend, John, Yoko. Keith Richard, Mick Jagger, and Brian Jones at the TV Studios, Stonebridge Park, December 10, 1968.

▲ Paul McCartney chats to American photographer Linda Eastman at the *Sgt. Pepper* press party London 19 May 1967. Linda who was in London on an assignment first met Paul four nights before at the Bag O Nails club.

▶ Press launch of *Sgt. Pepper* at Brian Epstein's house.

▼ Paul conducts a 41-piece orchestra during recording sessions for *Sgt. Pepper*.

> "I spent many hours and pounds on calls to the States. Fred Astaire was very sweet; Shirley Temple wanted to hear the record first; I got on famously with Marlon Brando, but Mae West wanted to know what she would be doing in a Lonely Hearts Club."
>
> *Wendy Hanson (Epstein's PA)*

By now so famous that they couldn't go unrecognized almost anywhere in the world, The Beatles changed the musical game again with their hugely influential concept album *Sgt. Pepper's Lonely Hearts Club Band*.

Still faithfully with George Martin as producer and the Parlophone label, this time the recording was at the Regent Sound Studios as well as Abbey Road and took place mostly during long night–early morning recording sessions (as The Beatles preferred). But this time the recording was much more indulgent and took between early December 1966 and late April 1967. A large orchestra and a huge range of musical styles were employed.

Starting from an idea of Paul's to develop an album of themed songs, the result was confidently experimental and explores a variety of musical approaches and instruments. Two of the songs ("Lucy in the Sky With Diamonds" and "A Day in the Life") were banned by the BBC for implied drug use, a position denied by the band at the time but later pretty much admitted.

The innovative album cover was done by rising pop artist Peter Blake and his wife Jann Haworth and showed The Beatles wearing colorfully extravagant military-style uniforms surrounded by a collage of over 70 famous figures both alive and dead. They included Marlene Dietrich, Marilyn Monroe, Edgar Allen Poe, Aleister Crowley, and Shirley Temple (twice), as well as many others. The inner gatefold shows a portrait of the band in colorful uniforms made by the theatrical costumier M. Berman Ltd of London.

SGT. PEPPER'S LONELY HEARTS CLUB BAND

Side 1
1 "Sgt. Pepper's Lonely Hearts Club Band"
2 "With A Little Help From My Friends"
3 "Lucy In The Sky With Diamonds"
4 "Getting Better"
5 "Fixing A Hole"
6 "She's Leaving Home"
7 "Being For The Benefit Of Mr. Kite"

Side 2
1 "Within You, Without You"
2 "When I'm Sixty Four"
3 "Lovely Rita"
4 "Good Morning, Good Morning"
5 "Sgt. Pepper's Lonely Hearts Club Band (Reprise)"
6 "A Day In The Life"

"Sgt. Pepper's Lonely Hearts Club Band is the most important rock & roll album ever made."

Rolling Stone magazine

Produced by George Martin for Parlophone, *Magical Mystery Tour* was recorded between late April and early November 1967 and released late November in the US and early December in the UK—just in time for Christmas sales. It was recorded at the Abbey Road Studios and the Olympic Studios in London. Many different musicians and singers contributed to the album.

However, only six new songs were available—recording of the title song started under a week after they finished *Sgt. Pepper*—so it's hardly surprising that there was not a lot of material for the project. The result was that this was too short for an LP, but too long for an EP—so they eventually decided on a double EP presented in a gatefold sleeve with an accompanying 28-page booklet of lyrics and photographs. It was released in various configurations for the different world markets: in the US stereo was added to the sound as well as five other versions of Beatles singles to pad it out to LP length. Also included was a bigger, better version of the booklet. This version sold better on import to the UK than the original did.

▶ The party takes tea en route.
▼ The Beatles set out on September 11, 1967.

154

MAGICAL MYSTERY TOUR

US version
Side 1
1 "Magical Mystery Tour"
2 "The Fool On The Hill"
3 "Flying"
4 "Blue Jay Way"
5 "Your Mother Should Know"
6 "I Am The Walrus"

Side 2
1 "Hello, Goodbye"
2 "Strawberry Fields Forever"
3 "Penny Lane"
4 "Baby You're A Rich Man"
5 "All You Need Is Love"

“An intriguing psychedelic companion piece to *Sgt. Pepper*, containing some fantastic material from The Beatles' hippy heyday ...”

Neil McCormick (Daily Telegraph)

Magical Mystery Tour (TV film)

Magical Mystery Tour developed from an idea of Paul's while on a trans-Atlantic flight from San Francisco back to London. He came up with a semi-documentary showing The Beatles meeting ordinary people as they journeyed on a mystery tour of southwest England by coach. Unfortunately, nothing "magical" happened on their journey and the resulting film was dull. In fact, much of it was shot at the recently disused RAF station at West Malling in Kent and most of the scenes shot around Devon and Cornwall were lost in the final cut. "The Fool on the Hill" was shot in the south of France near Nice.

This was also the first project for the new Apple Corps. and was in part designed to cheer up The Beatles after the death of Brian Epstein. It was shot between September 11 and 25, 1967.

The 52-minute long, largely unscripted film was primarily directed by Paul around a number of sketch situations only loosely hung together by the coach narrative. The film was shot in color but was shown in black and white on the monochrome-only BBC1 and then repeated a few days later in color on BBC2 after Ringo complained directly to the BBC about the original transmission. It was not broadcast in the US until the 1980s. The film features six new Beatles songs and premiered on the BBC1 on December 26, 1967. It was not critically well received despite featuring some great performances including "Death Cab For Cutie" performed by The Bonzo Dog Doo-Dah Band in a London strip club.

Written by and starring The Beatles, the cast included an eclectic mix of British character actors/comedians including Ivor Cutler as Buster Bloodvessel and Jessie Robins as Aunt Jessie, as well as various friends and Beatles crew members. Neither John nor George were enthused by the project and both did their best to avoid getting involved. Over ten hours' footage was shot and John later was only partly joking when he called it, "The most expensive home movie ever made".

▶ The Beatles in the studio in Soho finishing their film *Magical Mystery Tour.*

▼ George, John, and Neil Aspinall during filming of *Magical Mystery Tour.*

157

The Beatles was the first release from Apple Records, but thanks to its stark white cover with only a discreetly embossed title, the album is much more widely known as "The White Album." The first pressings were also numbered and have become very desirable collectors' items.

The White Album consisted of 30 new songs, mostly by Lennon/McCartney but also with four from George and one from Ringo. As usual, George Martin produced the album. It includes some of their best-known songs and was recorded between the end of May and mid October 1968 at the EMI Abbey Road Studios and at Trident Studios in Soho, London for four songs that needed their eight-track machine.

The plain white cover was designed by Richard Hamilton, a leading British pop artist, and it could not have been in greater contrast to *Sgt. Pepper*'s busily colorful cover. It opened up to a gatefold of portraits taken by John Kelly, and a large poster showing a collage of various pictures both formal and informal of The Beatles on one side and the song lyrics on the other.

The recording was marred by the bickering and tension that were precursors to the band's implosion.

THE BEATLES (AKA THE WHITE ALBUM)

Side 1
1 "Back in the USSR"
2 "Dear Prudence"
3 "Glass Onion"
4 "Ob-La-Di, Ob-La-Da"
5 "Wild Honey Pie"
6 "The Continuing Story of Bungalow Bill"
7 "While My Guitar Gently Weeps"
8 "Happiness Is A Warm Gun"

Side 2
1 "Martha My Dear"
2 "I'm So Tired"
3 "Blackbird"
4 "Piggies"
5 "Rocky Racoon"
6 "Don't Pass Me By"
7 "Why Don't We Do It In The Road?"
8 "I Will"
9 "Julia"

Side 3
1 "Birthday"
2 "Yer Blues"
3 "Mother Nature's Son"
4 "Everybody's Got Something To Hide Except Me and My Monkey"
5 "Sexy Sadie"
6 "Helter Skelter"
7 "Long, Long, Long"

Side 4
1 "Revolution 1"
2 "Honey Pie"
3 "Savoy Truffle"
4 "Cry Baby Cry"
5 "Revolution 9"
6 "Good Night"

On August 22, Ringo walked out on the band feeling excluded and fed up with all the waiting around as the others argued, leaving Paul to play drums on "Dear Prudence." Ringo went to Sardinia where he wrote "Octopus's Garden" (it would appear later on *Abbey Road*). After the others begged him to come back, he returned to the studio two weeks later.

Tensions also increased due to the invariable presence of Yoko Ono in the studio, and the appearance of the other wives and girlfriends. Previously, non-participating onlookers were discouraged from the studio. More than ever they were each exploring their own musical paths and few of the tracks have all The Beatles contributing; many are virtually solo efforts with other musicians for support. The result is a wildly varied album both in quality and style.

The working title for the album was "A Doll's House" but they had to drop it when another band used a similar name for their album. (*Music in a Doll's House* by Family). In spite of all the internal problems *The White Album* was well received by most critics and sold well worldwide going to No.1 on the UK album charts for seven weeks over the Christmas period and topping the US album charts for nine weeks.

> "And I came back and it was great, 'cuz George had set up all these flowers all over the studio saying welcome home. So then we got it together again. I always felt it was better on the White one for me. We were more like a band, you know."

Ringo Starr

▶ Paul playing drums during sessions for *The White Album*. He played the drums while Ringo was away on "Back to the USSR," "Dear Prudence," "Why Don't We Do It In The Road?," "Wild Honey Pie," and later, "The Ballad of John & Yoko."

BREAKUP
1969-70

"I never intended the statement to mean I'd quit ... When I saw the headlines, I just thought, Christ, what have I done? ... no one wants to be the one to say the party's over."

Paul McCartney

◀ The Beatles perform live on January 30, 1969.

Timeline

1969

January 2—the sessions that will result in *Let it Be* and "Get Back" start at Twickenham Film Studios.

January 10—George walks out. They all meet two days later but nothing is resolved. On the 15th they meet again and agree to George's proposal that they move back to Apple's Savile Road studios.

January 13—US album release, *Yellow Submarine* on Capitol. It reaches No.2, spends 25 weeks on the charts, and is certified gold on February 5.

January 17—UK album release, *Yellow Submarine* on Parlophone. It reaches No.3 and spends ten weeks on the charts.

January 20—the four Beatles meet at Savile Row where Magic Alex has been setting up a studio. It's awful and they have to borrow machinery from Abbey Road.

January 22—Billy Preston, who the Beatles knew from Hamburg, was invited to join the sessions on keyboards.

January 28—Allen Klein, who had been managing the Rolling Stones

▶ George and Pattie Boyd leave Esher and Walton Magistrates Court, March 18, 1969.

▶ Peter Sellers and Ringo at the wrap party for *The Magic Christian*.

affairs, met the band. George, John, and Ringo agreed to his involvement. Paul instead proposed his future father-in-law, John Eastman.

January 30—The Beatles gig on the roof of the Apple building is their last live appearance as a band. Billy Preston joins them for the 42-minute show.

February 2—Yoko's divorce from Anthony Cox is finalized.

February 3—Ringo begins filming *The Magic Christian* at Twickenham Studios with Peter Sellers. Allen Klein becomes The Beatles' business manager with John Eastman on Apple's General Counsel to keep a watching brief.

February 24—A merchant bank gets control of NEMS Enterprises.

March 12—Paul and Linda (four months pregnant) get married at Marylebone Register Office; witnesses are Mike McCartney and Mal Evans. On the 16th they fly to America for two weeks. George and Pattie are busted by the notorious Sgt. Norman Pilcher. They are found guilty and fined on the 18th.

March 20—John and Yoko fly to Gibraltar, get married, and fly to Paris—as described in "The Ballad of John and Yoko."

March 24—John and Yoko have lunch with Salvador Dali.

March 25—John and Yoko begin their Bed-in for Peace at the Amsterdam Hilton Hotel.

March 31—Apple press office sends out acorns for peace to world leaders.

April 11—Apple/Parlophone release "Get Back"/"Don't Let Me Down" which spends six weeks at No.1 and 17 weeks on the charts. Worldwide it will sell over four million copies.

April 14—John and Paul record "The Ballad of John And Yoko"— Ringo is still filming and George is abroad.

May 4—John and Yoko buy Tittenhurst Park in Sunninghill, Berkshire. They move in on August 11. Filming *of The Magic Christian* finishes. Ringo and Peter Sellers hold a party in London, John, Yoko, Paul, and Linda attend.

May 5—Apple/Capitol release, "Get Back"/"Don't Let Me Down" in the US. It spends five weeks at No.1 and is certified gold on May 19.

May 9—The Beatles row over Klein. Paul holds out. John, Ringo, and George leave Paul to record "My Dark Hour" with the Steve Miller Band. Zapple experimental record label is launched with two albums *Unfinished Music No.2: Life With*

The Lions by John and Yoko and George's Electronic Sound. The former is released in the US on the 26th.

May 24—John and Yoko fly to the Bahamas where Ringo and Maureen are on holiday … and then on to Canada on the 25th.

May 30—Apple/Parlophone release "The Ballad of John and Yoko"/"Old Brown Shoe." It spends 14 weeks in the charts, three weeks at No.1 from June 14.

June 1—in Toronto John and Yoko

▲ John and Yoko introduce the world to bagism.

▶ George at a meeting of the Krishna Temple Buddhists in London August 28, 1969.

record "Give Peace a Chance."

June 4— "The Ballad of John and Yoko"/"Old Brown Shoe" released in the US. It is banned by a number of radio stations in the US because John uses the word "Christ." The banning by some radio stations certainly affects sales and it can only make No.8 on the charts.

◀ John, Yoko, George, Pattie, Ringo, and Maureen in the audience watching Bob Dylan at the Isle of Wight Pop Festival.

It still sells over a million and is certified gold on June 16.

June 29—John, Yoko, her daughter Kyoko and John's son Julian go to Scotland. On July 1 they have an motoring accident that sees them all detained in hospital.

July 1—Paul rings George Martin to get him to work on the new album (which will be *Abbey Road*).

July 3—Ringo and Maureen stand in for John and Yoko at a launch party for "Give Peace A Chance."

July 4—Apple releases "Give Peace A Chance"/"Remember Love" by The Plastic Ono Band in the UK. It's released in the US on the 7th.

August 8—*Abbey Road* cover photograph taken. John contacted a photographer friend of his and Yoko's, Iain MacMillan, and at 11.35am, takes photos of the group walking across a zebra crossing, while a policeman holds up traffic.

August 9—the Manson murders.

August 20—the final mix of *Abbey Road* is the last day all four were together in a recording studio.

August 28—Paul and Linda's daughter Mary is born.

August 31—George, Pattie, Ringo, Maureen, John, and Yoko go to the Isle of Wight festival to watch Bob

Dylan perform on September 1.

September 13—The Plastic Ono Band play at a Toronto festival. The line-up is John, Yoko, Eric Clapton, Klaus Voormann on bass, and Alan White on drums.

September 22—*Northern Star* (an Illinois University newspaper) publishes the rumor that Paul is dead, citing clues on the cover of *Sgt. Pepper* and the words "I buried Paul" in the fade-out of "Strawberry

▲ John at Apple headquarters sending his MBE back to The Queen. November 25, 1969.

Fields Forever." The rumors are heightened by the *Abbey Road* cover photograph where Paul is barefoot and in black.

September 20—John says he's leaving the band.

September 26—*Abbey Road* released in the UK on Apple/ Parlophone. Hard to believe

1970

January 3 and 4—Paul, George, and Ringo's last sessions together on the *Let It Be* soundtrack at Abbey Road.

January 15—John's Bag One lithograph exhibition opens in London.

January 26—John writes and records "Instant Karma" with Phil Spector; George plays lead guitar.

January 30—John's interview with *Rolling Stone* is published and The Beatles split is made apparent.

February 4—John and Yoko meet Malcolm X, the Black Power leader.

February 6—The Plastic Ono Band's "Instant Karma (We All Shine On)" is released in the US with a Yoko Ono Lennon B side "Who Has Seen The Wind." It goes out in the US on the 19th.

February 11—John and The Plastic Ono Band record an appearance on *Top Of The Pops*. John pays the fines of 96 anti-apartheid protesters arrested at the South Africa-Scotland rugby match

February 26—*Hey Jude*, a collection of material unreleased

that the last album could be so successful: 81 weeks on the charts, 17 at No.1, it sells five million copies in its first year.

October 1—*Abbey Road* released in the US on Apple/Capitol, the first at a new royalty rate negotiated by Klein. Awesomely successful it spends 129 weeks in the charts, 11 at No.1, and is certified diamond on January 10, 1997.

October 6—"Something"/"Come Together" released on Apple/Capitol in the US. Another No.1, it also certifies platinum (in 1999).

October 20—"Cold Turkey"/"Don't Worry Kyoko (Mummy's Only Looking For A Hand In The Snow)" released by the Plastic Ono Band in the US. It comes out in the UK on the 31st.

October 27—Ringo starts work on *Sentimental Journey*.

November 25—John returns his MBE to Her Majesty the Queen as a protest against "Britain's involvement in the Nigeria-Biafra thing, our support of America in Vietnam, and 'Cold Turkey' slipping down the charts."

December 2—George joins the Delaney and Bonnie tour.

December 10—Ringo, Maureen, John, and Yoko attend the premiere of *The Magic Christian*.

December 12—The Plastic Ono Band's *Live Peace In Toronto* is released in the UK.

December 31—George, Pattie, Paul, and Linda see in the new year at Ringo and Maureen's; John and Yoko are in Denmark.

◄ John on February 11, 1970, performing with the Plastic Ono Band on *Top Of The Pops*.

◄ John on February 11, 1970, performing with the Plastic Ono Band on *Top Of The Pops*.

at No.6, spends two weeks at No.1, sells two million, and is certified platinum in 1999.

March 12—George and Pattie move to Friar Park in Henley-on-Thames.

March 19—*Top Of The Pops* shows a clip from *Let It Be*.

March 23—Paul finishes mixing his solo album, *McCartney*.

March 27—Ringo's *Sentimental Journey* is released.

April 1—Phil Spector records a 50-piece orchestra at Abbey Road for *Let It Be*.

April 10—Paul's press release announces he has left The Beatles.

May 8—the album *Let It Be* released in UK on Apple/Parlophone. It spends three weeks at No.1, 59 weeks on the charts.

May 11—the Beatles' last US single, "The Long And Winding Road"/"For You Blue," released on Apple/Capitol. It reaches No.1 on June 13, spending two of its ten weeks in the charts at the top.

May 13—the movie *Let It Be* premieres in New York.

May 18—the album *Let It Be* released in the US. It spends four weeks at No.1, has over

on album before (including "The Ballad of John and Yoko," "Revolution," "Lady Madonna," and "Paperback Writer") comes out as an album in the US on Apple/Capitol as *Apple*. It spends 33 weeks on the charts, sells three

million in four months, and is certified platinum in 1991.

March 6—The Beatles' last single "Let It Be"/"You Know My Name (Look up my number)" is released on Apple/Parlophone. It reaches No.2. In the US, it enters the charts

four million sales, and is certified platinum in 1997.

May 20—the movie *Let it Be* premieres in the UK in Liverpool and London.

November 27—George's single "My Sweet Lord"/"Isn't It A Pity" released in the US. It will come out in UK with B side "What is Life" on January 15, 1971.

November 27—George's triple album, *All Things Must Pass*, released in the UK. It comes out on November 30 in the US.

December 11—John releases the album *John Lennon/Plastic Ono Band*.

December 26—George becomes the first Beatle to have a solo No. 1 hit when "My Sweet Lord" reaches the top in the US.

December 31— Paul instigates proceedings to bring The Beatles to an end.

▲ Paul's press is headline news, April 10, 1970.

66 The saddest thing was actually getting fed up with one another. It's like growing up in a family. When you get to a certain age, you want to go off and get your own girl and your own car, split up a bit. 99

George Harrison

Linda Eastman
September 24, 1941–April 17, 1998

Linda Louise Eastman was born in New York into a wealthy Jewish-American family. She was married at 21 to a fellow college student at the University of Arizona in June 1962 and had a daughter, Heather Louise, with him in December that year. She became interested in photography and started taking pictures of rock stars when she became the house photographer at the Fillmore East concert hall in the East Village, New York City.

In May 1967 she traveled to London, officially on assignment to photograph "Swinging London," but secretly hoping to meet Paul McCartney, which she did at the Bag O'Nails club in Soho on the 15th. Four days later they met again at Brian Epstein's house in Belgravia for the launch party of *Sgt. Pepper* and then she had to return to New York. At this time Paul was still with Jane Asher and supposedly not a free agent.

They met again in New York in May 1968 when John and Paul announced the launch of Apple Corps. and they properly became a couple. They married at Marylebone Register Office on March 12, 1969, when Linda was four months pregnant with their daughter Mary. Hundreds of fans turned out to see them; Paul was 26 and Linda a year older. They went on to have two more children, Stella and James, and formed the core of the band Wings together.

Linda did not get blamed as much as Yoko for the break up of The Beatles, but she did receive hostility from many fans. She died of breast cancer in 1998 at the age of 56.

▶ Paul and Linda were married on March 12 at Marylebone Register Office. Heather is in front; Mal Evans at left of image.

Yoko Ono
February 18, 1933–

Yoko Ono was born into a wealthy Japanese banking family. As a teenager she spent time in New York where she liked to mix in artistic circles and soon developed into a performance artist. She had divorced twice and in her second marriage had a daughter, Kyoko.

Enormously influenced by her friend and frequent collaborator John Cage, Yoko became an avant-garde conceptual and performance artist and film-maker working mostly from New York. She met John at the Indica Gallery in London in November 1966 where some of her works were being exhibited. She later claimed that she had never heard of The Beatles. Although John was still married to Cynthia, they started seeing each other. Their affair continued until John divorced Cynthia in late 1968. The other Beatles were not as enthralled as John by Yoko—and neither were the majority of his fans, many of whom blamed her for their break up.

As "The Ballad of John and Yoko" relates, they married in Gibraltar on March 20, 1969, and honeymooned in bed in Amsterdam campaigning for peace. On April 22, 1969, John changed his name by deed poll to become John Winston Ono Lennon. In 1969 they performed in Toronto as The Plastic Ono Band and released their first album, *Live Peace in Toronto 1969*.

John and Yoko had a son, Sean, in 1975. Yoko was returning home to the Dakota Building, New York, after a recording session at Record Plant Studio with John on December 8, 1980, when he was shot dead by a fanatic. He was cremated in New York and Yoko took possession of his ashes.

▲ John, Yoko, Julian, and Kyoko on holiday in Scotland, July 2, 1969.

173

YELLOW SUBMARINE

Released on Apple Records *Yellow Submarine* is the soundtrack to the eponymous animated cartoon and includes six new Beatles songs—four from John and Paul, and two from George—and an additional seven instrumental tracks from the George Martin Orchestra. Produced by George Martin, the new songs were recorded at Abbey Road and the De Lane Lea studios in central London between May 1967 and February 1968. The album appeared in the UK seven months after the film was released.

The album had patchy sales and was not as well received as previous Beatles albums. It did not top the charts in either the UK or US, although it still sold well by any other bands' standards. Of course, the catchy song "Yellow Submarine" had already been a big No.1 as a double A-side single with "Eleanor Rigby" back in 1966.

The artwork for the cover is done in the same psychedelic style as the film and shows the four cartoon Beatles standing on top of a hill while other characters from the film, including the yellow submarine, surround them.

Yellow Submarine (film)

Director: George Dunning
Released: by United Artists July 17, 1968

The Beatles were under contract to make one more film for United Artists, and just before he died Brian Epstein had signed them up to make a musical animated feature-length film. They all had deep reservations about being represented in cartoon form, so they refused to have anything to do with it; they were also still hurting from the critical mauling that *Magical Mystery Tour* had received.

Side 1
1 "Yellow Submarine"
2 "Only A Northern Song"
3 "All Together Now"
4 "Hey Bulldog"
5 "It's All Too Much"
6 "All You Need Is Love"

Side 2
*Music by George Martin
and Orchestra as played in the film*
1 "Pepperland"
2 "Sea of Time"
3 "Sea of Holes"
4 "Sea of Monsters"
5 "March of the Meanies"
6 "Pepperland Laid Waste"
7 "Yellow Submarine in Pepperland"

> "Years later, 'Yellow Submarine' remains the gateway drug that turns little children into Beatle fans, with that cheery singalong chorus."
>
> *Rolling Stone magazine*

►John, George, and Paul recording for *Yellow Submarine*.

They refused to voice their own characters and didn't want their songs used—until, that is, they saw how brilliantly and originally the movie was animated. They changed their minds and even agreed to appear in the epilog. However, other actors still voiced The Beatles characters and various British character actors contributed their voices to the other animations.

The concept for the film was developed from the song "Yellow Submarine" previously released on *Revolver*. Over 200 artists worked for eleven months to animate the film under the psychedelic style art direction of Heinz Edelmann who created the look of the movie under the general direction of George Dunning.

The film was a box office hit with its very of-the-moment graphics and soundtrack and its peace and love conquers all philosophy. The film is full of puns, in-jokes, sly imagery, and British cultural references. The animators even echoed the ways each of the Beatles moved so they have a distinct and recognizable character of their own. As with anything to do with The Beatles all manner of interpretations have been ascribed to the film and its meanings, most of them completely wrongly.

In the end all The Beatles were delighted with the film.

►Paul, Ringo, and George pose with a cardboard cut out of John from the *Yellow Submarine*.

ABBEY ROAD

The last of the studio albums was *Abbey Road*, recorded, of course, at their familiar studios with George Martin producing, but this time for the Apple label.

All of the tracks were written by The Beatles and were recorded between February and August 1969. It went straight to the top of the UK album charts where it stayed for 11 weeks, dropped to No.2 for a week, and then returned to the top for a further six weeks. Across the Atlantic, it hit the top after three weeks and stayed there on and off for 11 weeks in total. By 1980 *Abbey Road* had logged ten million sales worldwide.

The album cover photograph shows the four Beatles walking across a zebra crossing on Abbey Road. There is no lettering to show the name of the album, nor the band. The photo was taken on August 8, 1969, just before midday by Scottish photographer Iain MacMillan, a friend of John and Yoko.

Abbey Road was recorded back on familiar territory in a deliberate attempt to capture the way they used to work together and to put their many differences behind them. Although it wasn't actually stated, each Beatle knew in his heart of hearts that this was in all likelihood their last album together. They had already quarreled badly during the uncompleted sessions for the *Let It Be* album and this was an attempt to clear the air. Immediately after recording finished, John was working with The Plastic Ono Band and had mentally if not physically left The Beatles.

Side 1
1 "Come Together"
2 "Something"
3 "Maxwell's Silver Hammer"
4 "Oh! Darling"
5 "Octopus's Garden"
6 "I Want You (She's So Heavy)"

Side 2
1 "Here Comes The Sun"
2 "Because"
3 "You Never Give Me Your Money"
4 "Sun King"
5 "Mean Mr. Mustard"
6 "Polythene Pam"
7 "She Came In Through The Bathroom Window"
8 "Golden Slumbers"
9 "Carry That Weight"
10 "The End"
11 "Her Majesty"

“ *Abbey Road* lays out its terms precisely and meets them all. There's not a duff note on the damn thing. ”

Mark Richardson (Pitchfork.com)

▶Immortalized on album, today's street sign is in a different form to that on the cover but covered in graffito.

By January 1969 Paul had managed to convince the other Beatles to record an album reminiscent of the old days when their sound was raw and unpolished. He was anxious for the group to perform live again and for that they had to get back together and play again—for this, a new rock and roll album was the answer. All the songs were their own compositions except the traditional Liverpool folk song "Maggie Mae."

Rehearsals for the album started at Twickenham Studios as the plan was to film the making of the album. But after rehearsing and recording for about a month they quit the project and just left the tapes for future use. They had quarreled continuously throughout the sessions; George had even quit for a week and driven home to his parents in Liverpool—he only returned when the others agreed to move the rehearsals away from Twickenham. He then also brought in Billy Preston to help out. It was a relief to everyone when they finished.

George Martin and Glyn Johns worked on the first sessions but The Beatles did not like the results and George Martin withdrew from the project after some hurtful personal criticisms. Johns remixed the tapes but still no one was happy. The tapes were stored away and left untouched for a year during which time The Beatles recorded *Abbey Road*. Finally, after a year Phil Spector was brought in to remaster them—John was happy with the results but Paul, in particular, was not. He hated what Spector did to his songs, especially "The Long and Winding Road."

The album was finally released on the Apple label in May 1970 by which time The Beatles had broken up. The album sold well on both sides of the Atlantic but the professional critics were mostly unimpressed, generally feeling that Phil Spector was not stylistically the right producer for The Beatles.

LET IT BE

Side 1
1 "Two Of Us"
2 "Dig A Pony"
3 "Across The Universe"
4 "I Me Mine"
5 "Dig It"
6 "Let It Be"
7 "Maggie Mae"

Side 2
1 "I've Got A Feeling"
2 "One After 909"
3 "The Long And Winding Road"
4 "For You Blue"
5 "Get Back"

"Forty years ago this weekend, the greatest band of all time gave the world their final album together: On May 8th, 1970, the Beatles released *Let It Be*."

Daniel Kreps (Rolling Stone magazine, May 7, 2010)

177

Let It Be (film)
Director: Michael Lindsay-Hogg
Released: 8 May 1970

Filming started at Twickenham Studios in January 1969 when the film was originally entitled "The Beatles Get Back," and intended for a television documentary. The decision was taken for financial reasons to turn it into a theatrical release. The early shots are of the band rehearsing and working out melodies in studios that proved cold, vast, and lacking in atmosphere. The band and crew moved to the Apple Corps. basement and slightly better conditions. Designed to show how The Beatles worked together to create an album, instead it is an uncomfortable watch of a band quarreling and falling apart. The cameramen took hundreds of hours of film and were so ubiquitous in the studio that the principals soon forgot they were there. The result is some truly raw footage: The Beatles themselves did not want the film released, but the accountants won.

The highlight is the unexpected rooftop performance on January 30 on the roof of 3 Savile Row, Mayfair, London. During the impromptu gig somebody called the police to complain about them disturbing the peace. The intention was for The Beatles to be arrested (great cinema verité) but instead the police only asked them to stop.

Phil Spector remixed the album but was not engaged at the time of filming so does not appear. The film with its original soundtrack won the Academy Award for Best Soundtrack (accepted by Paul) but the album uses Spector's interpretations. John was happy, Paul wasn't—it has been suggested that this was one of the principal reasons why The Beatles broke up.

◀ Closeup of John and Paul during the live gig on top of the Apple building.

Apple Corps.

Apple Corps. was founded in 1967 to represent The Beatles and all their business interests and to replace their earlier company, Beatles Ltd. The headquarters are at 3 Savile Row, London, where The Beatles famously performed unannounced on the roof on January 30, 1969.

The company initially came about purely for tax reasons because The Beatles had two million pounds in their accounts that had to go to the taxman or else be invested in a business venture. Paul came up with the name inspired by René Magritte's painting of a green apple. Just as the company was being set up, Brian Epstein died causing complete upheaval of The Beatles in every way. But his death was the catalyst for the band to take personal control of their own financial affairs.

They decided to form their own record label for their own music (instead of using NEMS) and to take on other worthwhile artists. Apple Corps. Ltd. became official in January 1968 and the Apple trademark (designed by Gene Mahon) was registered in 47 countries. In February they extended their range by registering in five distinct areas: records, film, publishing, retail, and electronics as Apple Music Publishing, Electronics, Retail, Management, Films Ltd., Publicity, Overseas, Records, Tailoring Civil and Theatrical.

On May 14, 1968, John and Paul launched their concept at a press conference in New York, the latter explained, "We are in the happy position of not needing any more money. So for the first time, the bosses aren't in it for profit. We've already bought all our dreams, we want to share that possibility with others."

▶ Fans cluster round for goodies on the last day of opening of the Apple Boutique.

Billy Preston
September 2, 1946–June 6, 2006

▶ George and Billy Preston
perform in Landover, Maryland
on December 13, 1974.

William "Billy" Preston was born in Houston, Texas. He was quickly spotted as a child prodigy when he started playing the piano at the age of three and by the time he was ten he was playing the organ on stage with gospel singers like Mahalia Jackson.

In 1962 Billy was 16 and touring Germany working as Little Richard's organist. He met The Beatles at the Star Club in Hamburg. Years later in 1969 when The Beatles were arguing over *Let It Be,* George walked out in disgust. One evening he went along to a Ray Charles gig in London with Eric Clapton but he didn't recognize Billy playing the piano until he was introduced: he had grown a lot bigger in the intervening years. After the gig George sent a message inviting Billy to the Abbey Road studios. George said, "I knew the others loved Billy anyway, and it was like a breath of fresh air … Just bringing a stranger in amongst us made everybody cool out."

Everybody behaved themselves and Billy played piano on several sessions and joined The Beatles for their impromptu rooftop gig. The single "Get Back" is credited as "The Beatles with Billy Preston," the only official joint credit The Beatles ever allowed. Partly by way of thanks for his help, Apple Records signed Billy to their label in 1969. *That's The Way God Planned It* was released in September 1969 and was produced by George Harrison, who also guested on it, as did Keith Richards, Ginger Baker, and Eric Clapton.

> " The Beatles did treat me as a member of the group. And that was a great honor, you know? "
>
> *Billy Preston*

▶ Ringo with George and Billy Preston, October 9, 1990.

THE BEATLES

LEGACY

"We did have big fights, but we still loved each other. We split up, and it was about time. But there was still lots of contact."

Ringo Starr

◄ Beatles' fans gather to observe a ten-minute silence for John Lennon, shot the week before in New York, December 1980.

After The Beatles

Following the split of The Beatles, the four never got together as a band again, although upon occasion some of them collaborated together. They had been in each other's pockets and as close as brothers for years, both before their fame and throughout the existence of The Beatles, and as in many families, small quarrels became magnified. The Beatles were constantly asked to reunite, something they said they would never do … and any possibility of a reunion ended when John was shot dead in 1980.

None of The Beatles ever needed to work again, because their music had made them wealthy, but still the music-making urge drove them. They all produced solo albums and played new music, but they also explored other career avenues and interests: for a few years John became a house husband looking after his son Sean; Ringo became involved in acting; and George almost by accident became a film producer with his production and distribution company HandMade Films, which notably rescued the Monty Python film *Life of Brian* from financial collapse.

John was already making music with his lover Yoko Ono during the last months of The Beatles. Similarly, Paul started the band Wings in which his wife Linda was an essential part. In 1971 John and Yoko moved to New York City where they set up home, but as John was noisily critical of US involvement in the ongoing Vietnam War, the Nixon administration repeatedly attempted to deport him. For fear of not being allowed back into the US, John could not travel abroad: this severely limited opportunities to meet his ex-band mates.

John remained close to Ringo, but his relations with Paul and George fluctuated, compounded by

▲ An inflatable yellow submarine at the entrance of the Beatlemania exhibition in Hamburg, May 28, 2009.

▶ Beatle memorabilia is still avidly collected.

▶ Beatles' fans outside the HMV music store in Liverpool, waiting to buy the new *The Beatles Rock Band* interactive computer game and digitally remastered albums, on September 9, 2009.

George's dislike of Yoko. John was hurt by George's autobiography, which barely mentioned him, and they were estranged at the time of his death. With Paul he had a three-year slanging match through the press and attacked him in the song "How Do You Sleep?" They did meet up a couple of times and appeared to be coming round to a reconciliation before John was shot—he was recording new music on the day he was murdered. Not long before he died John said, "I still love those guys. The Beatles are over but John, Paul, George, and Ringo go on."

George was always the most spiritual of The Beatles and he immersed himself in Indian culture and music even more after the demise of The Beatles. In 1970 he released the triple solo album *All Things Must Pass*. In 1971 George organized the Concert for Bangladesh to raise money for flood victims. George continued to work musically; he wrote three hits with Ringo, played on John's *Imagine* album, and worked with a wide range of musicians including The Traveling Wilburys, comprising George, Jeff Lynne, Bob Dylan, Roy Orbison, and Tom Petty. George died

▲ Actor Eric Idle, Billy Preston, and Ringo Starr attend a gala screening of "The Concert for Bangladesh Revisited with George Harrison and Friends" on October 19, 2005, in Burbank, California.

◄ George at the Gary Moore concert at the Royal Albert Hall in London October 1992.

of lung cancer in California on November 29, 2001. His ashes were scattered in the River Ganges.

Paul, however, has been the most successful ex-Beatle and has been acclaimed as "the most successful musician and composer in popular music history." His output since The Beatles speaks for itself and he is treasured on both sides of the Atlantic.

▶Paul had been married twice—to Linda Eastman and Heather Mills—before Nancy Shevell. Here the happy couple after their October 9, 2011, wedding.

▼A sad and solitary John in 1970.

187

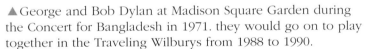 George and Bob Dylan at Madison Square Garden during the Concert for Bangladesh in 1971. they would go on to play together in the Traveling Wilburys from 1988 to 1990.

◄ L–R: Paul, Linda, Olivia Harrison, Barbara Bach, and Ringo in November 1984.

▶ John and Yoko in 1971, the year they moved to New York.

What's on the DVD

The DVD packaged with this book has three sections: one is a real oddity (or should that be Doddity?). It's a 15-minute mock interview of The Beatles with Ken Dodd, a fellow Liverpudlian, a comedian and a singer of no little merit: "Tears" spent five weeks at No.1 in 1965. Then there's a 20-minute 1966 documentary about The Beatles tour of America and the furore caused by John's "more popular than Jesus" comment. The main feature is an hour-long documentary, following a diary format, that mixes newsreel and TV footage to provide a fascinating glimpse of The Beatles' life. It is divided into sections whose contents includes:

1. Rise to Fame
The birth of Beatlemania; includes footage of the band leaving for a tour of Sweden on October 23, 1963.

2. Rattle Your Jewelry
An interview about the Royal Variety performance. Footage of the band meeting the Queen Mum; of The Beatles going to a gig in a Police Black Maria; and a Christmas 1963 interview.

3. Conquering Western Europe
On January 14, 1964, The Beatles flew to France: footage of their departure and arrival; of reaction to "le yeah yeah"—what the French called their music; and their return to the UK.

4. American Beatlemania
The groundbreaking first US tour: interview before the trip; departure from Heathrow and arrival in New York; press conferences in US and on the band's return to the UK.

5. Growing Wealth
A discussion about wealth and meeting Cassius Clay[George's 21st birthday and the filming of *A Hard Day's Night*.

6. Variety Club
On March 19, 1964, at the Dorchester lunch receiving their Variety Club Personalities of the Year awards; footage of the event and their acceptance speeches.

7. First World Tour
With Ringo in hospital suffering from tonsillitis, drummer Jimmy Nicol joined the band as they left for Denmark on June 4, 1964; an interview with Ringo out of hospital; scenes of the arrival in Australia and the huge crowd at in Adelaide. Back in UK they attend the London and Liverpool premieres of *A Hard Day's Night*. Then they embark on another tour of the US.

8. Beatles for Sale
Returning from US, Ringo's back in hospital to have his tonsils out and interviewed as he went in and came out and after Xmas he married Maureen Cox on February 11, 1965.

9. Acknowledgements and Awards
Awarded MBEs in 1965, there's an interview with Paul and Ringo when it was announced and interviews after receiving their medals; footage of Paul receiving Ivor Novello Awards; George and Pattie get married on January 21, 1966.

10. "Damn Beatles Go Home"
A quote from a Japanese politician did not hamper a Japanese tour; but they had a bad experience in the Philippines as their post-tour interview shows. The section includes coverage of their last tour of the US, an interview with John about the "more popular than Jesus" remark; and an interview with a hooded Klu Klux Klansman.

11. Going Solo
The first dawnings of a life outside the band are discussed in interviews with John, Paul, and Ringo as they arrive at Abbey Road while recording *Sgt. Pepper*. There's footage of Paul discussing LSD in 1967.

12. All You Need is Love
Footage of the band's involvement with the Maharishi opens this section; followed by a glimpse of the Beatles and their wives as they attended the memorial service to Brian Epstein on October 17, 1967; then footage of the band going to see the premiere of John's *How I Won the War*. 1968 sees a chat with Paul and George about *Yellow Submarine* and an interview with Paul and Linda on their marriage.

13 John and Yoko
The final section starts with footage of John and Yoko after they got married; and then there's a chat from their honeymoon bed in Amsterdam.

Photo Credits

Many thanks to the organizations who supplied images, specifically to David Scripps of Mirrorpix and Sean Harry of Getty Images. This listing provides page/image reference number/credit.

2/3 00267966 Mirrorpix, 4/5 00123410 Mirrorpix, 6/7 00267572 Mirrorpix, 8/9 86202271 K & K/Redferns/Getty Images, 10/11 73906761 Michael Ochs Archives/Getty Images, 12 86203852 Ellen Piel/K & K/Redferns/Getty Images, 13 90730595 SSPL/Getty Images, 15 91146996 Mark and Colleen Hayward/Redferns/Getty Images, 16 89874629 Mark and Colleen Hayward/Redferns/Getty Images, 17 73908837 Michael Ochs Archives/Getty Images, 18 89876501 Jürgen Vollmer/Redferns/Getty Images, 19 103457148 Nigel Osbourne/Redferns/Getty Images, 20 3374828 Keystone/Getty Images, 21 107425293 Keystone-France/Gamma-Keystone via Getty Images, 22T 84884674 David Redfern/Redferns/Getty Images, 22B 86203854 Ellen Piel/K & K/Getty Images, 23 102624623 Nigel Osbourne/Redferns/Getty Images, 24 73908620 Michael Ochs Archives/Getty Images, 25 89876520 Jürgen Vollmer/Redferns/Getty Images, 26 120059121 Michael Ochs Archives/Getty Images, 27 102169563 Nigel Osbourne/Redferns/Getty Images, 29 74253750 Michael Ochs Archives/Getty Images, 30 106558169 K & K Ulf Kruger OHG/Redferns/Getty Images, 31 85347760 GAB Archive/Redferns/Getty Images, 32 85842590 Jürgen Vollmer/Redferns/Getty Images, 33L 89876473 Jürgen Vollmer/Redferns/Getty Images, 33R 89876455 Jürgen Vollmer/Redferns/Getty Images, 34 86203471 K & K Ulf Kruger OHG/Redferns/Getty Images, 36 89876506 Jürgen Vollmer/Redferns/Getty Images, 37 BE025847 Bettmann/Corbis, 38/39 00263180 Mirrorpix, 40 136401110 Keystone/Hulton Archive/Getty Images, 41L 86202755 K & K Ulf Kruger OHG/Redferns/Getty Images, 41R 86202275 K & K Ulf Kruger OHG/Redferns/Getty Images, 42L 120362424 TS Productions/Getty Images, 42R 106626204 RDImages/Epics/Getty Images, 43L 85348468 GAB Archive/Redferns/Getty Images, 43R 107425354 Keystone-France/Gamma-Keystone via Getty Images, 44 104402186 Keystone-France/Gamma-Keystone via Getty Images, 45 78971779 Popperfoto/Getty Images, 46 57590275 Blank Archives/Getty Images, 47 00179730 Mirrorpix, 48 74284963 Michael Ochs Archives/Getty Images, 49 3280198 Keystone/Getty Images, 50 74286835 Michael Ochs Archives/Getty Images, 51 112058656 Harry Hammond/V&A Images/Getty Images, 52 00268021 Mirrorpix, 53 78960794 Popperfoto/Getty Images, 54 74001422 Michael Ochs Archives/Getty Images, 55 85235252 Fiona Adams/Redferns/Getty Images, 56 86201960 Max Scheler/ K & K/Redferns/Getty Images, 57TL 00103244 Mirrorpix, 57BL 00103300 Mirrorpix, 57R 00102534 Mirrorpix, 58 91141364 John Rodgers/Redferns/Getty Images, 59 00337408 Mirrorpix, 61 00084579 Mirrorpix, 62 UT0094280 Reuters/Corbis, 64 85234794 Fiona Adams/Redferns/Getty Images, 65 3425368 Chris Ware/Keystone/Getty Images, 67 U1412269 Bettmann/Corbis, 68/69 2638882 Ted West & Roger Jackson/Central Press/Getty Images, 70 3141269 Pace/Getty Images, 71 00268245 Mirrorpix, 72 00346735 Mirrorpix, 73T 00268228 Mirrorpix, 73B 00268231 Mirrorpix, 74L 00180307 Mirrorpix, 74R 00266863 Mirrorpix, 75 00268007 Mirrorpix, 76 00269787 Mirrorpix, 77L 00268252 Mirrorpix, 77R 00268214 Mirrorpix, 78 00189146 Mirrorpix, 79 00337404 Mirrorpix, 80 00354106 Mirrorpix, 81 00264849 Mirrorpix, 82 00106607 Mirrorpix, 83 00268433 Mirrorpix, 84 00354496 Mirrorpix, 85 00268436 Mirrorpix, 86/87 00264881 Mirrorpix, 88 00276587 Mirrorpix, 89 00264857 Mirrorpix, 90 00179701 Mirrorpix, 91 00264851 Mirrorpix, 92 00192495 Mirrorpix, 93 00179762 Mirrorpix, 94 104588238 Daily Express/Archive Photos/Getty Images, 95 74274557 Michael Ochs Archives/Getty Images, 96T 3297170 Keystone/Getty Images, 96B 00180325 Mirrorpix, 97 86202935 Max Scheler/K & K/Redferns/Getty Images, 98 00268220 Mirrorpix, 99 00179689 Mirrorpix, 100 00179754 Mirrorpix, 101 00276570 Mirrorpix, 102 00180322 Mirrorpix, 103 00192497 Mirrorpix, 104/105 00268178 Mirrorpix, 106 00084835 Mirrorpix, 107 3430034 Mirrorpix, 109 90730600 SSPL/Getty Images, 110 00180204 Mirrorpix, 112/113 00268180 Mirrorpix, 114 00264472 Mirrorpix, 115 00371965 Mirrorpix, 117 74253739 Michael Ochs Archives/Getty Images, 118/119 51240034 Getty Images, 120 102726251 Manchester Daily Express/SSPL/Getty Images, 121 74253272 Michael Ochs Archives/Getty Images, 122T 00268188 Mirrorpix, 122B 00164987 Mirrorpix, 123T 86203850 K & K Ulf Kruger OHG/Redferns/Getty Images, 123BL 86202424 K & K Ulf Kruger OHG/Redferns/Getty Images, 123BR 03296690 Keystone/Getty Images, 124 3280200 Keystone Features/Getty Images, 125 00082357 Mirrorpix, 126 91139140 Cummings Archives/Redferns/Getty Images, 127 3167331 George Stroud/Express/Getty Images, 128/129 3137526, 3137649, 56171544 all Larry Ellis/Express/Getty Images, 130 74253267 Michael Ochs Archives/Getty Images, 132 00180188 Mirrorpix, 133 00268246 Mirrorpix, 134 73989136 Michael Ochs Archives/Getty Images, 135T 85348269 GAB Archive/Redferns/Getty Images, 135B 3133616 Harry Benson/Express/Getty Images, 136/137 00180352 Mirrorpix, 138 107425374 Keystone-France/Gamma-Keystone via Getty Images, 139 00179761 Mirrorpix, 140 00103277 Mirrorpix, 141 2665767 BIPs/Getty Images, 142 00179122 Mirrorpix, 143 86202422 K & K Ulf Kruger OHG/Redferns/Getty Images, 144 0180376, 00180408 both Mirrorpix, 145 73874340 Hulton Archive/Getty Images, 146 104047919 GAB Archive/Redferns/Getty Images, 147 00264916 Mirrorpix, 148 00162363, 00170445 both Mirrorpix, 149 00102518 Mirrorpix, 150TL 00103158 Mirrorpix, 150TR 00179760 Mirrorpix, 150B 3232180 Larry Ellis/Express/Getty Images, 152/153 00268700 Mirrorpix, 154 00268176 Mirrorpix, 155 00277920 Mirrorpix, 156 89843270 WireImage/Getty Images, 157 00146156 Mirrorpix, 159 85238566 Tom Hanley/Redferns/Getty images, 160/161 00114729 Mirrorpix, 162 00164968 Mirrorpix, 163 00165253 Mirrorpix, 164 107425314 Keystone-France/Gamma-Keystone via Getty Images, 165 00059094 Mirrorpix, 166 00180272 Mirrorpix, 167 00059127 Mirrorpix, 168 00284339 Mirrorpix, 169 83981463 Mirrorpix, 170 83049004 Mirrorpix, 171L 00264541 Mirrorpix, 171R 104478934 RDImages/Epics/Getty Images, 172 80747690 Getty Images, 173 00114451 Mirrorpix, 175T 3296486 Keystone Features/Getty Images, 175B 00179017 Mirrorpix, 176 42-16360066 Beth A. Keiser/Corbis, 178 00085568 Mirrorpix, 179 91143200 John Rodgers/Redferns/Getty Images, 180 110527231 Time & Life Pictures/Getty Images, 181 3450534 David Hume Kennerly/Getty Images, 182/183 00165371 Mirrorpix, 184 88029288 Krafft Angerer/Getty Images, 184 inset 85234025 GAB Archive/Redferns/Getty Images, 185 93430839 Paul Ellis/AFP/Getty Images, 186L 00264893 Mirrorpix, 186R 55968497 Amanda Edwards/Getty Images, 187L 00165005 Mirrorpix, 187R 00364855 Mirrorpix, 188 00179735 Mirrorpix, 189L 92923748 Bill Ray/Time & Life Pictures/Getty Images, 189R 00180205 Mirrorpix.